Journey Into
The Unknown

Journey Into
The Unknown

Cora murray

DECEMBER 2012.

Margaret Rutherford

To order additional copies of this book, contact:
Xlibris Corporation
0-800-644-6988
www.Xlibrispublishing.co.uk
Orders@Xlibrispublishing.co.uk
305001

Introduction by the Author

My life prior to meeting Alexander in 1960 is another story. I feel, however, that I have to give you just a little idea of where I came from and how I got to the stage in life I am relating to you. I had what you would call a very middle-class childhood. My dad was a ladies' hairdresser, and my mother was at home. She hadn't worked since their marriage in 1926, when she was employed as a shorthand typist in a shipping office. They would not have classed themselves as 'working class' as that was for manual workers. I was sent to ballet classes, piano lessons, Sunday school, and Brownies and then Guides. My father was an elder in the Church of Scotland and sang in the choir when I was young. My mum just liked to be at home, looking after my dad, brother, and myself from 1936. We lived in a council house, in a very nice part of Dundee. You have to remember in the 1930s there were not many people who actually owned the house they lived in. Dundee was like a lot of Scottish towns, full of tenements which, in some cases, were in a terrible state. However councils were beginning to build houses fit for people to live in. The only drawback for the council—could the people afford to live in them? The rents were often beyond the purse of the working man. Most of people who were living in my area worked in offices or for the council in various positions, or they had businesses of their own. Our immediate neighbours included a policeman, an office worker who was a town councillor, and a manager of a public house. I had been educated at the local primary school and, having passed my eleven+, went to the Harris Academy. I had the aspiration to be an art teacher or to work in a magazine as an artist; however, I was unable to get my Higher English. I was sent to a private commercial college, just like my mum, and went to work as a junior in Timber Merchant. The front door of the office could be seen by my mother from the kitchen window through the gardens of the houses on the other side of the street. It took all of three minutes to get to work. I moved up the ladder and eventually was taught how to work an NCR accounting machine. I left to take up a position in town with a state-owned fuel supplier. Eventually, by the time I met Alexander, I was in a position where I was in charge of two of these machines. I looked after the private ledger, salaries, stock, and cheque writing. We also did the wages and hire purchase, which was in its infancy, and the cash and cheque sales. The customers' accounts were done in a different department on a different type of machine.

I was in Girl Guiding as an assistant Guide leader, called a lieutenant, with camping qualifications and a Brown Owl leader of the Brownies for our church companies. I enjoyed Guiding very much—working with the girls and camping. I was chosen to attend the 1957 World Guide Camp at Windsor as one of three adult leaders representing Dundee. I was also a prospective adult leaders trainer for the Brownie Section. I had not been short of boyfriends, and I was quite sure of myself and enjoyed life. I had a number of friends I socialised with. I liked nice clothes and had the money to buy expensive outfits. Like a number of young people in the late 1950s, I did have problems at home. Life had moved on, but my parents were of a generation who had not. I learnt to only tell them what I knew they would approve of and kept the rest to myself. My dad being a ladies' hairdresser, I was able to have my haircut etc., as often as I wanted, by the young apprentices in the shop. Dad had, by this time, sold his shop and was working as manager of the salon in Draffens of Dundee. I had a number of boyfriends from the age of sixteen, but only three were what we termed 'serious', meaning that the relationships had lasted many months or even years. My last had ended after three years with heartache for me. My parents were against him and gave me an ultimatum to choose between him or them. They said I wouldn't be happy with him etc., etc. At that time, girls just didn't have their own flats and certainly didn't leave the home until they were married. Students and nurses lived in accommodation given to them in students and nurses homes. I had nowhere to go, so I gave in and finished the relationship. It was at this point in my life that I met Alexander.

What did I look like? I had fair hair, with various depth of colour, helped, of course, by my visits to see the apprentices in the salon. I was five feet three inches tall, very slim, not beautiful, but had blue eyes and small nose and mouth. I dressed well, and I suppose I would be called an attractive girl.

Why did I want to write this story? My reason for writing this story—which has taken many years to develop and a great deal of searching into my memories and which had lain dormant in the recesses of my mind—is twofold. I have met women who have married into the merchant navy with all that it entails. I have met others who have lived in Iran. I have known families who have experienced the death of children. I met others who lived with cystic fibrosis. I have seen television programmes of children being treated in Great Ormand Street Hospital, where my eldest daughter was treated. I know of lots of people who have adopted children for one reason or another. I have, however, never met anyone who experienced every one of these except me and all of it in a ten-year span of life.

The second is simple; if you met me you would never think that anything untoward had happened in my life. I am a half-cup-full person, who leads a very happy and active life in the community that I have made my home for the last thirty-five years. That tragedy did not stop with the end of this story but struck again for myself and my two lovely children in 1978 with the very sudden death of my beloved husband and their daddy at the age of forty-one. Those around me and known to me are aware of that, but very few have any idea of life between 1960 and 1970. Most of those who were very involved have died, but none of them really ever knew the real story.

This story is based on facts although, due to the time that has elapsed since it happened, names have been changed to keep their true identity private and because some have been forgotten. Also the places and times are as the author remembers them and may not be a true description in the eyes of others. The photographs in the book are owned by the author.

Prologue

'The mystic East!' exclaimed the owner of the small shop. 'How exciting and romantic!' The owner was like her shop—small and compact and dressed as if she had put on all her jewellery and scarves. Her dress was black and her hair grey and tied in a knot on top of her head. The shop sold everything for ladies, from pins and needles to clothes. Margaret had gone in with her toddler, May, her new baby, Margaret, and her mother-in-law, who was sure that Mavis's shop was bound to sell cotton underwear. Margaret was having a problem finding these items as most were now made from synthetic materials. Her mother-in-law had explained to Mavis that the family was about to travel out to South Iran. Margaret wasn't sure about the 'mystic East' or the 'romance', but she was excited about living in another country and being with her husband as a family. However, we have to go back even further in time to 1960 so Margaret can tell you the whole story.

Chapter 1

April 1960

I suppose, looking back, Alexander, or 'Alex' to his friends and family, arrived in my life when I needed someone who thought me special. I know that my close friends thought I was just going out with him because he had a car, money, and good looks. I don't know if that is true or not; probably at the beginning it was. After the trauma of a previous relationship, it was nice to feel that you were special again. I met Alex, who came from, at that time, a small town on the east coast of Scotland. He lived with his mum and his dad and younger brother Alastair. We met one night at a private dance some two months after my break-up from that long-term relationship. It was a Rugby Club Dance, and I had gone with one of my friends, Isabel, just for the night out. Alex happened to be there. I remembered him from a few years ago when he had shown an interest in a friend, but he had disappeared off the scene. He had, in fact, joined the merchant navy and had completed his apprenticeship with one of the oil companies, on oil tankers as an engineer. He asked if he could take me home that night, and we were inseparable for the next six weeks. How can I describe Alex? Six feet tall, with broad shoulders but slim hips; wavy, fairish hair, very fine in texture; blue eyes; and I thought him quite good-looking. He was quiet and well mannered with a very pleasant nature and a good sense of humour. He was attending the Technical College in Dundee, taking part of the 'Ticket'. I learnt that was what the qualifications for marine engineers and masters were named. He very quickly took me to meet his mother. I was given instructions regarding how and where we met prior to the visit, not at a dance as that would have been frowned on. Poor Alex had the same problems at home as I did and kept most of his life a secret from his parents. I found his mother quite charming, very polite and precise. She was a good-looking woman—quite tall with white hair; although she was in her early fifties. He looked like her but wasn't, I am glad to say, anything like her in nature. I then brought him home to meet my parents. One of the things that attracted me to Alex was his whole life. He lived in much the same atmosphere as I did in some respects. He understood about my inability to communicate with my parents regarding anything that they didn't approve of, and that was quite a lot. It is common knowledge that young people in the 1950s and early 1960s had a far rougher time than the young people today; most parents were still living in the world as they knew it, which was a hangover from the Second World War. Their values and way of living were quite different from the life the young people wanted to live. I decided, before he came to the house, that this time I would not allow my parents to come between Alex and me, and that if I wanted to take the relationship forward, I would, and nothing and no one would stop me. We saw each other every day and enjoyed each other's company. We went away in the car visiting different towns at the weekends, had nice meals in the evening, and in general, had a good time.

My mum and dad gave me no indication whether they did or did not like him, though my mum appeared to be very fond of him. He went to the football matches with my dad and his friends. We visited my brother Patrick, who, by this time, was married to Alice. My mum and dad were really not altogether for Alice. It may be that she had led, from what I could gather from her, a different life from mine and Patrick's. My parents wouldn't like anyone who was in any way different; they couldn't make head or tail of her life and Patrick was not forthcoming, so most of it was guesswork. I knew some of her life because she told me, but I would not repeat any of it to my parents. One of the problems my dad had at that time was trying to pass a driving test. He bought his first car in his fifties when he owned his own hairdressing business. At that time my brother and Alice were living in Dundee and he had the job of ferrying Dad everywhere. This was a bone of contention as Dad and Mum liked to go out for a drive on a Sunday afternoon and Patrick had to take them. Alice preferred to stay at home, and that was one of the many things that went against her. Eventually, when the Suez crisis of the late 1950s came along, my dad ended up with a license when all the learners who had a provisional of more than six months got one. He was always a bad driver. It was your life in his hands!

However, all good things come to an end, and at the end of six weeks, in May 1960, Alex had to go back to sea. I was unhappy to see him go, but after such a short time, I could not commit myself to anything. He said that he would love to take me on a holiday when he came home but I probably wouldn't go unless we would be married! I said I wouldn't. I suppose that was the nearest to a proposal he could do under the circumstances. I did promise him that I would never send him a 'Dear John' letter and that I would wait until he came home before I decided one way or another.

Chapter 2

May 1960, Scotland

Life went on as usual for me the year Alex was away. I enjoyed visiting the Dundee Repertory Theatre ever two weeks with my special friends. There were at that time still young men interested in me, and I was tempted only once to go out with a young man I often saw when at the Rep. However, I was not interested and it was a one-off. I gradually stopped going dancing on Saturday nights and often spent them with Patrick and Alice.

Alex and I wrote every week, and I was sent flowers at Christmas. I went every Tuesday to visit his mum and dad. As time went on, I began to see the kind of person his mum was. She complained a lot about other people. She thought it was important to look correct and behave in a certain way. Appearances were very important. She had friends but was disparaging about them behind their backs. I began to think that maybe she was jealous in some way. She was born and brought up in Glasgow in a family of three boys and three girls. She had the same background as my parents had. Some made good, some didn't. My father-in-law was my favourite. I can't remember when she told me that Dad had had an affair when they lived in Glasgow. I don't know if the affair was before Alex's brother Alastair's birth or just after. It is immaterial when it was because it dominated her life from then on. I never knew any woman who looked and acted as if life was not good. She always seemed to be unhappy about something, and it usually concerned Dad. Even at the beginning I felt sorry for him. They had a lovely flat, well furnished, and much more superior in furnishing than my mum and dad's. Yet she was not happy and always harked back to what she had in the beginning.

From what I was told by my mother-in-law, father-in-law's family had owned a large soft furnishing and household goods shop in the centre of Glasgow. Grandfather was the head of the business. He had three children; the eldest a son was a chemist and had nothing to do with the business. My father-in-law and his twin sister, Morag, both worked in the shop. Morag was in the office and father-in-law on the shop floor. He learnt the trade in Lewis's in Glasgow before joining the family firm. My father-in-law's family—Mother, Father and the children—were comfortably well off and lived in a large house outside Glasgow. When he married Mother-in-law, a house was built for them in a small village far enough outside Glasgow to attract those who could afford to build in the 1930s. They had everything new, everything they wanted, everything that money could buy. Alex came along in 1936 and Alastair, five years later. Alex went to Hutchison's Grammar School in Glasgow. Unfortunately, the business was sold off after the death of Grandfather, when Alex was about twelve or thirteen years. Life from that point seemed to have gone downhill. The first thing they did was to buy a large country house in Perthshire and had a go at the 'good life'. Father-in-law had a job as a salesman for, I think, a soft furnishings firm; then he bought a fishmonger's shop in Dundee; however, that was not a success. If it had been a fish and chips shop, it may have done better, but not fresh fish! By the time I met them in 1960, they were probably at the lowest point financially but seemed to be all right by themselves; they had a small soft furnishings business next to their flat, and he worked for a large company in Dundee.

I heard about Alex's birth more times than I can remember, and it always came back to the hard times and how she was told not to have any children for a while. They had been Plymouth Brethren at that time. If you do not know about them, they are, I think, a very strict sect, like Jehovah's Witnesses. By the time I met Alex, they were members of the Church of Scotland. I got to know her very well that first year, but she was very careful with me as I was not yet married to her son.

Chapter 3

Spring 1961, The Past Catches Up

Whenever I visited Alex's mum and dad, I went by train after work. One night when I arrived at the station in Dundee on my way home, I found the young man I had finished with prior to meeting Alex waiting for me. He took me to the bus stop, and our conversation was mainly about him to begin with. Then he started to meet me at the office every Tuesday and take me to the train as well. Over the intervening weeks, he told me about his girlfriend and how he would marry her if I didn't take him back and similar. I started going by bus and didn't see him for a while. One evening, he was outside the office as I was finishing and he asked me if I would visit his mum as she was in Dundee Royal Infirmary. I was very sad as I realised that she was dying of cancer and had asked if she could see me. I was very glad I went and I was able to hug her and hold her hand and speak to her of her son and listen to her wishing that he was with me. She was very tired but not in pain. It made a very big impression on me and lived with me for a very long time. Two days later, I saw the announcement of her death in the papers. I could not tell my mum and dad about the visit, so I was unable to go to the funeral.

As life would have it, about that time, my very first proper boyfriend telephoned me as he had returned from India, where he had worked for two, two-year terms. He invited me for a meal, and I went along mainly out of curiosity. He was very full of his time in India and all he had seen and done. He was hoping to go into a business, but for the meantime, he was at home living with his mum and dad. I knew that all the indications were that if I was willing, he wished to renew our friendship. I wasn't the girl he knew at eighteen years and he was not the young man I knew, and although he was very nice and I wished him well, I had no desire to start again. I think that I had, by this time, decided that I really liked Alex very much and he was the one for me if things were the same when he came home. I knew there wouldn't be any hassle from my parents, and I could have a life that would be my own.

Very shortly after that, Alex wrote in his weekly letter that the tanker he was on was arriving at South Shields for dry dock. He would not get leave immediately but would have to go on standby for at least three weeks. This was in April 1961, and he had been away since May 1960. Once he got to South Shields, he spoke to me by phone every day and we arranged that I would go down there and live on the tanker for a long weekend at the beginning of May. He made arrangements with the captain so that I could have the state room next to the captain's suite for my personal use. His boy (servant) would be on hand to look after all my needs when Alex was on duty. I spent three wonderful days on board the ship. It was an oil tanker, not a luxury liner. A bit careworn but clean. All the furnishings in all the oil companies' tankers are made of the same material and of the same colours. I was looked after by his boy so well that he slept outside my door every night and was on guard all day when we were on board, hovering about to make sure I was OK. We laughed a lot about that time in later years. The expectations on Alex's part were thwarted by an over-diligent servant. Well, I was quite happy he was diligent as I wanted everything to be perfect. Alex looked really great, all tanned from his journeys and so pleased to be with me.

I was met at the station on my return by his dad and mum and went off to their home with all the gifts from him to them. In the eleven months he had been away, he had visited South America, Japan, and Australia to name but a few countries. They were waiting for me to tell them I was engaged, but we had decided to wait until he came home. When I got home that night to Dundee, my mum and dad were also expecting me to say we were engaged.

Chapter 4

An End to the Old Life

Our life together really began at this point, and even by now it was different and, somehow, it never was anything else. It is just as well we cannot look into the future.

He arrived home on the 18 May 1961, and his dad and I met him at the station and took him home. He distributed all the gifts be had collected for us and had a meal. He borrowed his dad's van to take me home. I was glad we had had the weekend in South Shields as a year away from each other is a long time when you are young. We did not feel awkward in each other's company, and I felt as if I had known him for a long time. We decided then to get married as soon as possible. The next morning, the 19 May, he asked my dad for permission to marry me, and my dad gave a cheeky answer, 'I thought I would never get her off my hands, and one thing I can tell you, life with her will never be boring.' We went off to Dundee to select the ring and have lunch, and we talked about the future. We had decided we wanted to be married during his leave, which was three months, so we picked the middle Saturday, which was the 24 June 1961, as our wedding day.

Our wedding was not a very large affair, mainly because we had only six weeks to make all the arrangements. We did the main planning in that first weekend; my dad saw the minister about the church, and we had to find a hotel. We had, of course, chosen one of the busiest weekends in the year, midsummer. The main reason for the size was the difficulty in getting a large enough hotel for all the guests we wanted. The Ballinard Hotel in Broughty Ferry was able to squeeze in seventy-six guests and the bridal party. I loved nearly every part of those six weeks and, of course, the day itself. I visited his grandmother in Dunning and his relations in Glasgow to be 'shown off'. I took him to meet my godmother, Dr M. C. Campbell, and other family members in Dundee and St Andrews. Alex's mum began to show her real colours, and that was really the start of my realising just what she was like. I did give her all the information on what was happening, but somehow her face always registered displeasure. My dress was bought in a Dundee shop called Alice Adair but had to be specially made in London as I was so slim (thin) that none of the shops had a dress to fit me. It was white brocade with a rose pattern embossed through it. The bridesmaids, Helen and Isabel, who had been friends for nearly four years and my two best unmarried friends, who believe it or not are still friends to this day, were beautiful in their turquoise dresses—one having very dark hair, almost jet-black and the other glowing auburn.

I think that some of the things that stand out in my mind from that time were happy and some showed how life was in both our families' lives. Alex had the usual stag night. Before the night was out, his friends cut off all the buttons on his waistcoat. The style at that time for young men was waistcoats with their tweed jackets and cavalry trills and brown suede shoes when out on the town. He could not ask his mum to sew them on, as she would have disapproved and given him a hard time. He brought it to me to sew them on again. In a pub, drinking was a terrible thing for him to do! My hen night was quite different. The girls in the office dressed me up as a bride with a veil and a long dress. There was a potty with a baby in it and a bunch of flowers made up of cauliflower. I received a gift from the staff on the Tuesday evening, which happened to be my birthday. That presentation itself was a lot of fun as one of the men had written a poem. Then all the girls in the office met up with my friends outside the office and walked me through the centre of Dundee. We went home in a public transport bus and walked up the terrace I lived in. Alex was hanging out of the kitchen window, watching the crowd of laughing and singing women bringing me home. My mum had laid on a lovely buffet for us all. We had a great night. Mum, Dad, and Alex sat in the kitchen until all the girls left. The next two days were taken up with showing all the lovely gifts that we had received.

On the night before the wedding, we had a rehearsal in the church, and my mum took down all the flowers to arrange in the church. She went around everyone's gardens in the terrace who had offered flowers to get enough. It was decided after the rehearsal that the young people, Helen, Isabel. Alec, Martin—the best man—and Neil, Isabel's boyfriend, would, along with Alex and me, go for a meal into town. The reason was to let everyone in the bridal party meet each other before the big day the next day. We had a very happy time, and we weren't late as we all had to get home on the buses and trains. When I arrived home, my father was in one of his terrible rages. Where had I been? Why was I out so late!? He flung off his tailcoat into one corner and his trousers into another and said the wedding was off. As you can imagine, I was so very upset. I telephoned my brother to tell him what was going on, and he said for me to stick it out only one more day and he would come out of it by the morning. I couldn't forget that night for a long time. I know my dad was probably upset that I had not gone straight home with them after the rehearsal and spent the evening with them, but he knew where I was and I wasn't late, about 10 p.m. He ranted and raved about all that my mum had to do for me and said I should have been there to do it myself. Of course, my mum had nothing to do for me that night; it was already done. What she was doing was getting herself and him ready. I suppose it was his way of showing he was still in charge, and he was in reality upset at my leaving home but just couldn't convey it to me in any other way. It had been decided that after an initial six weeks in a rented flat belonging to schoolteachers, I was to stay with them until at least Alex's next leave, when we intended buying a house, so I wasn't leaving home for good yet.

The other thing that stands out was the look on my mother-in-law's face when she saw my wedding dress. It was lovely and flattered my slim figure. It was empire line gathered under the bust with a smooth panel down the front. There was gathering on the hips and a train starting under a bow on the back. My veil was a short one, and I had a pearl headdress. My bouquet was red roses and white lily of the valley. The girls had bouquets of lemon roses. All my mother-in-law cared about that day was that everything should be just so, and it was. By this time, my mum and dad felt that she really didn't think I was good enough for Alex and that the wedding day wouldn't be up to her standards!

I can remember everything I did that Saturday and I knew that I was going to enjoy my special day, and I felt like a princess. One of our neighbours, Mrs Landsmen, came in and helped me dress and saw my dad was OK and locked up the house after us. When I left the house, all the neighbours were outside with the younger children to see me off and to shout 'Good Luck' etc. I had lived in that house since I was six weeks old, and I was twenty-five years old four days before my wedding. Of course, the wedding was beautiful, and I knew the minister so well through my involvement with the Sunday school and the Guiding. When we were about to leave the vestry after signing the register, he said with a lovely twinkle in his eye, 'Don't run down the aisle. We know you are so happy to get your man but just take your time.' The reception a very happy, friendly affair, as it should be. I did feel lovely and so happy and loved Alex so much. At the end when the guests were leaving, one of mother-in-law's friends came up and, in front of everyone, thanked my mum and dad for a wonderful day and said that there was no way that they (her husband was at her side) could ever give their daughter such a lovely wedding. My mother-in-law's face was like thunder. We had bought tickets to a private dance in Broughty Ferry near where the reception was held for all the young people to finish their day. At that time, the receptions stopped at about 8.30 p.m. partly because the bars closed at 9.30 p.m. in Scotland in those days.

Chapter 5

A Whole New Life

When we left the reception at about 8 p.m., we got into my dad's car, lent to us for the week—he could be very kind when he wanted to be. We drove to Pitlochry Hydro Hotel in Perthshire, arriving at about 9 p.m.

We had booked into the Pitlochry Hydro for two nights. We arrived after the dinner was served, but of course as life would have it, the head waiter had recently arrived from a hotel in Forfar that we used to frequent when we were courting and knew us quite well. After our initial embarrassment at him realising that we were on our honeymoon, we were able to get a meal, only the two of us in a huge dining room. At least it appeared to be very large that night. We had just got into the bedroom when a knock came to the door, a telephone call for Alex. No telephones in the rooms, not even in the best hotels in 1961. So off he went down the stairs at breakneck speed to hear my dad's voice at the end of the phone.

'Are you all right? What are you doing?' Alex managed to say all the right things, like we arrived safely and we had had supper and were now putting on coats to go for a stroll in the moonlight!

'Enjoy yourselves and goodbye,' said Dad. My brother tells me how it was the only time he ever saw our dad under the influence of alcohol. My mum and dad and Alice and Patrick, after the reception, went for a meal, having eaten about 4 p.m. and it now being around 8.30 p.m. They had gone by taxi into Dundee, and my dad kept telling the taxi driver that they were celebrating his daughter's marriage. Well, of course, the taxi man thought Alice was the daughter, which would have been OK, but Alice was noticeably pregnant and it was 1961.

By the time they got home, my dad was adamant that he was going to phone and make sure I was all right. None of them would argue with him, so off he went to the phone and came back quite happy to tell them that I was all right. I suppose that answers part of the question about his irrational behaviour the night before. We had a good laugh as we recalled the story from our point of view. Alex had just started to undress and had to scramble into his clothes again. He used to say, 'You would have thought the old man could see over the miles and through the walls.'

We had a lovely honeymoon except for the Scottish summer—rain, rain, and more rain. We travelled to Inverness, then on to the Isle of Skye, then up to Ullapool, and then back to Inverness. Then we spent one night in Glasgow at his aunt's, then back home. 'Home' for the next six weeks was the rented flat in Perth Road belonging to three teachers, who were all on holiday. We learnt to live with each other as young couples do. Alex didn't like me going off to work every morning and couldn't wait for me to get home at lunchtime. We were very sexually attracted to each other, and I have to admit I often wished I could just stay off work. I also found out that it was a culture shock for him to marry me after coming from a house kept by a house-proud mother. We soon got our routine sorted out, and while I was away, he did his bit around the house. I have to say it was the start of four very happy years for the two of us personally. We had our fair share of differences of opinion, but we never really had a major falling-out in all these years. When Alex left to go back to sea, I moved back in with my mum and dad. I missed him very much, but I knew that this was the life I had married into and so must make the most of it. Life went back to its usual routine—work, Guiding, meeting friends.

Chapter 6

A Sailor's Wife

It was a cold late-January morning, and I was looking my best, as one did in those days. There was no central heating, a coal fire in the bedroom only if you were sick, but your best bet was a hot-water bottle. I had on a pair of Alex's socks, thick pyjamas, and a cardigan, and that was me dressed for bed. Well, that was the picture I made that morning, when we had a surprise knock on the door. I could hear my mum's exclamation when she saw Alex standing there. She was all excited and went off to make a big breakfast; I got him into what was to become not 'my bedroom' but 'our bedroom'. How we clung together, but it wasn't the time for anything more. He tidied up before going into the warm kitchen for a slap-up meal. Then he turned to me and said in front of Mum and Dad, 'Well, wee wife, come along.'

The last I heard was my mum saying, 'Oh, John.' You would have thought I was a lamb going to be slaughtered. Nothing could have been further from the truth.

Alex went back to college to sit another part of his Ticket, so we got into a nice routine. Life at home was so different from what it had been before—chalk and cheese. I know Alex had a lot to do with that as my mum really liked him and he her. I think he had a real mother for the first time. My mum wasn't dressy, his mum was; my mum made a house a home, his mum made a house to look at. My mum didn't work; his mum helped his dad in his curtains etc. workshop next to their flat. My mum wasn't interested in trying to impress anyone; his mum was the opposite. My mum had a sense of humour.

By the end of March, I found out I was pregnant and everyone in both households was very, very excited at the prospect us of our having family. My mum and dad had a grandson, John, four months old, at that time, but Alex's brother, Andy, was some five years younger and although he had a few girlfriends, nothing serious. His mum had high hopes of one young girl, but her grandma didn't think Andy was good enough for her. That was a blow to my mother-in-law's ego and, of course, entirely father-in-law's fault. After all, he was the one who went through all the money with his rash ideas etc., not she with her expensive ideas!

Everything went well with the pregnancy to begin with, and then I began to feel very tired and lethargic. The doctor decided I should stay off work and rest for a few weeks as I was a bit anaemic. My mum had been talking to Alex one day, and they had been discussing a house for us. We started to go out in the evenings, always taking my mum with us. Alex would drive my dad round to the bowling green, and then off we would go on a house-hunt, to look at houses for sale in and around Dundee.

My brother and his wife, Alice, had a house on a new private housing estate in West Ferry, where houses were still being built. I loved the area and thought their house lovely but a bit more than we could afford. I got the all-clear to start my work again on the first Monday in June. I had been off work for three weeks and was nearly three months pregnant. On Saturday, I took my Brownies for their annual picnic to Carnoustie for an afternoon on the beach. We had a lovely time, and I felt great. When I got home, Alex had a surprise for me. He had laid down a deposit on a house to be built on the opposite corner of the next street to my brother. I would not be alone when he was at sea as our front door was diagonally across from their back door. I was so excited and couldn't wait until the next day, when we would all go to see the plot. On Sunday, we went off in the afternoon, visited my brother and Alice and baby, then walked up the road that was being laid to a piece of ground with six posts marking our semi-detached bungalow, ours being, in fact, the second house in but was to be built diagonally on the corner. It was to be ready in September, in plenty of time for the baby who was to be born in November. I was over the moon—a loving husband, a baby, and a house. My life was all coming together.

That evening, I had a sore stomach; it was just a niggle but enough to be annoying. I thought that maybe I had eaten something which did not agree with me. As the evening went on, it got worse, and when I visited the toilet, I noticed a spot of blood. Alex immediately phoned my doctor, and he said to go to bed and not to get up on any account. It was probably nothing but just to make sure. The pain got worse and worse, and I was unable to bear it. Alex said I looked like death; my colour was awful. In the end, I had to get up go to the toilet. I was extremely sick and had what I thought was diarrhoea. I was sitting on the toilet and being sick into a basin, both ends at the same time. I never had such excruciating pain in all my life, not even later in childbirth. My mum, who had had two children and had been given chloroform both times, had no idea what was happening to me. She was completely at a loss. Alex was distressed at the state I was in. I was exhausted. My mum flushed the toilet and cleaned up the mess, never thinking to look into the toilet bowl. I was sure I had lost my baby, but when the doctor came early the next day, he was adamant that I hadn't. I was, of course, not allowed to go back to work. Alex had exams to sit, and we just had to wait until the doctor thought it was safe for me to have an internal examination. I kept telling everyone I had had a miscarriage, but the doctor wouldn't let me back to work. I was putting on weight as I was not allowed to do a thing for myself. In fact, I was blossoming. However, just after Alex's exams and his departure to join his ship, I found out that I was right and that I had lost the baby that night. My mum was always sorry that she didn't look into the toilet bowl, but as they all thought I had eaten something, I did not blame her. I was upset at my loss and felt very down and lonely as Alex was away. I went and got a passport, just in case I got a chance to join him on a ship. He was working on a coastal tanker as he had been given a compassionate trip of three months and a promotion to Fourth Engineer. They were allowed their wives on board coastal tankers. He had passed part of his Ticket, hence the promotion.

The miscarriage taught me how fragile a hold we have on life. The sense of loss and grief that people have when they lose a baby through a miscarriage is just as great as any other. I remember very clearly how happy Alex and I had felt; we all were looking to the future, and how suddenly it had all been taken from us. It is different when one is faced with the dilemma of choice, to keep or abort a foetus, and because I never wanted that dilemma, I knew what I had to do later on in my life. I do agree with abortion and in particular when the health of the woman must come first; she should never be put at risk. I also feel that the life of the baby and the kind of a life he or she would have must be taken into account, especially any disability of mind or body.

Chapter 7

West Ferry, 1962

I soon got back to normality—work, Brownies, visiting my in-laws. I was really upset at my mother-in-law's attitude to my miscarriage. She had, of course, had one after Andy and said it was her daughter that she lost, although she actually had no idea what sex it was. Somehow she made me feel as if I had done it deliberately. I was learning to cope with her and her attitude. I have to say I really liked my father-in-law; he was very sympathetic about it all and gave me a big hug and said there will be other babies. Then he said something to make me laugh. They had a grand piano in their lounge, and Papa was a lovely singer. He had been in the Glasgow Male Voice Choir when they lived outside Glasgow. He used to play, and the pair of us would sing, or in my case, I would do my best.

Alex came home at the end of September, and we moved into our house in West Ferry at the beginning of October 1962. It was a wonderful time for me. My beloved Alex was with me, and I had my own wee home with all the furniture and wedding presents filling it. We had been busy buying the last things since he arrived home after being away for only three months. That is the shortest time he was away in the years he was at sea. We settled in and had a lovely leave. I just loved my house and my life. It was decided that I should give up my work before he came home as Alex didn't want me working when he was on leave. I became a lady of leisure, and I loved it. We were so happy, and life was good. Alex was at college again to resit part of his Ticket. He didn't do very much in the way of study, but by a miracle, he did pass some of the exams. I found out that I was pregnant just before Alex was due to join his ship. This time there were no problems with the pregnancy. I seemed to sail through it. When he left to join his next ship at the end of November he was made a Third Engineer on the results he had gained. Once again it was a coastal tanker, as Alex had requested, and he was given this ship due to my pregnancy and my history.

I was able to visit Alex on board his tanker when it came into Grangemouth. The Chief Engineer came from Monifieth and one of the young deck officers, John Macintosh, was from Glenrothes. The Chief's wife, Mildred, came and collected me, and then we drove to Glenrothes for Shona Macintosh. Shona and John had two daughters, a baby, Catherine, and a toddler, Milly. Milly came along, so we were a happy bunch. One of the most memorable visits was over the New Year. The tanker was sitting out in the harbour away from the jetty. It was absolutely dreadful weather with ice and snow. The whole ship froze; there was no water at all. We were lying in the bunk with my fur coat over us trying to keep warm, when this man's voice came resounding along the alleyway.

'Mr Moray, are you not aware that we all frozen? No water, Mr Moray.'

'No, sir, I have been asleep' was the reply. By this time, Alex was on his feet and scrambling into his clothes and out the door at full speed. I was left shivering in the bunk. We had to evacuate the tanker, and, shock of shocks, we had to go over the side and down a ladder into the rescue boat. I don't think I had ever been as embarrassed in my life as I was trying to get off the ship. I had one young deck officer putting my feet on the rungs of the ladder and another above me encouraging me down. The one putting my feet into each rung as we went down had his head up my skirt as it kept getting in the way. I have to admit it was only when I was in bed in a hotel in Grangemouth that it dawned on me.

Alex was home again in April when I was about five months pregnant. Every time he came home, it was a wonderful time—the anticipation and joy of seeing him again and being together. Apart from one weekend when we were to visit Carnoustie to meet Brethren friends of the Morays, life was good and very happy. We had gone down to have tea with them and no one was in when we got there, but we waited around as we expected them to return soon. However, they didn't, and by the time they returned, it was long past teatime and it was very plain that we were not meant to be there at all. We left saying nothing about tea and got the bus home. I was starving, and Alex was upset. It was the first of the many upsets we were to have regarding his mum. The boys always seemed to me to be unable to stand up to their mother or say anything against her, and I was always very careful what I said. I could see that she had let him down, so I wasn't going to make it worse. After all, he was the most important person in my life and I would not hurt him for the world. I was always very careful about his mum, but eventually, he did see her for what she was.

Alex had to leave just after our second wedding anniversary. His ship was in Newcastle in dry dock, and he phoned every day. At 4 p.m. I would 'waddle round to a neighbour's'; we had no phone at the time. I was always OK, and he missed me. My mum and dad came to stay a few weeks after Alex left when the birth was imminent. I was looked after well with Mum and Dad and Alice and Patrick around to help me.

Chapter 8

Mary Rose

I began to feel uncomfortable on Monday and couldn't put my finger on what it was. The previous Saturday I had made my mum a nervous wreck as I wandered around Dundee looking at the shops, but I wouldn't have been doing that by Monday afternoon. I said nothing to Alex as I waddled my way round to the neighbour's house at 4 p.m. All evening and all night I had this pain in my lower stomach. It reminded me of the miscarriage. The pain was similar but not too strong. By lunchtime on Tuesday, the pains were coming at regular intervals, and it was decided by Alice and Patrick that I should be taken to Maryfield Maternity Hospital by him on his way to his work in the afternoon. He was to be at the weekly farmers' market meetings and would be away from a phone, so off I went. No mobile phones in those days. The midwife was sure that it wouldn't be long before I was a mum. I was told to put on my nightdress but not to go to bed; I was told to walk about as much as I could. The pains were coming every few minutes and the birth seemed very imminent. The midwife did all the things one has to do before a birth. That was late on Tuesday afternoon. My brother visited me in the evening; I was allowed my male relatives as the father was away. I walked the corridors the rest of Tuesday evening into Wednesday. My mum and mother-in-law visited on Wednesday afternoon. As usual, my mother-in-law was her usual gracious self. Wondering why the baby hadn't been born, she was upset that it had not yet appeared. She was not half as upset as I was. I was still having very painful contractions, but my waters had not broken. Late in the evening, they took me into the delivery room and broke my waters. It was a long labour, and I was extremely tired. I could hear all the discussions going on as to whether I should be given a Caesarean. I am sure today I would have been given it without all the delay; however, the birth was in the end natural.

May Rose Moray was born on 15 August 1963, weighing in at 8lb 2oz. Little did I know that her birth was to change the lives of so many people or that neither Alex nor I would ever again be the people we were before her birth. Not right away, but over the next six years we were to experience so many things that other couples never know anything about and should be thankful that they don't.

Firstly, where did her name come from? We both liked 'May Rose', and that was the name chosen for her before she was born. First thing, a telegram arrived for me, which was opened by the Sister in case it was bad news, so she said. It was, of course, from Alex. Then flowers appeared from him, and, even better, he managed to get just an afternoon off on the Saturday after her birth. His ship was still lying in Newcastle and was to sail at twelve midnight. I wasn't told about it in case he didn't manage to get the time off. My friend, Helen, was desperate to tell me but had been told to keep quiet. He arrived just around teatime on the Saturday evening. My dad met him at the station, took him to their home where Mum fed him, and then he brought him to the hospital. After the visit, Dad drove him back to the station. Alex thought that she was beautiful, and I amazed him as I was sitting knitting when he came in, all hale and hearty. My only regret was, I didn't look my best, no glamour on; still, it was wonderful that he saw his lovely little daughter, and he called me 'My wee wife'. She was a lovely baby; well, aren't they all in their mother's eyes?

I breastfed her, and she made steady progress, never getting fat or thin, just going along beautifully. It was a busy time for me, alone with a new baby, but most enjoyable. She ate well and slept well. When she was about six weeks old, I had her christened. Helen was her godmother and May wore my father's christening robe. She was too big for it, but we managed to make it look as if it fitted. Babies in the last twenty-seven years must have grown bigger as my mum said it fitted me. The minister who married us, christened her.

I went down every Tuesday to visit Granny Moray. I walked about a mile downhill to the railway station at West Ferry. I had to travel in the guard's van as the large coach pram was too big for anywhere else. The journey going was OK, but in the evening, the walk back up the hill was another story. Quite often, Granny Moray would arrive at the house unannounced, all dressed for a visit to Dundee, hat, gloves, high heels. She would arrive about 9 a.m., walk in, go straight to the baby cot, lift her out, give her a cuddle, and walk around with her. Then after five minutes, she would walk out, leaving me with a crying baby. Pop would just coo and smile at May, while he waited for Granny to be ready to leave. She very rarely came to visit as such, but then she didn't need to; I did the visiting. My mum came to visit every week and had to change two buses to get to see me. Dad came after work, and once May was in bed, they went home. I often saw them on Sundays when Mum would bring lunch with her. They just loved being with me and helping me. In all my married life my mum and dad never came unannounced to my home; they only came when they were invited. They said that their home was my home, but my home was Alex's and mine.

Alex came home when May was four months old. He adored his little daughter, and we had our first Christmas as a family. We had a big party, as he had missed her christening, and life was just great. We didn't go down to his parents' as often as I did because of the weather. Sometimes Alex would get Dad's car to take us down. Sometimes his dad would drop his mum off and pick her up on his way home. It amazed me how she could do that when Alex was around but never when he was away. I never, of course, said a word, and I suppose at that time Alex thought that his mum was in the habit of visiting and that it was normal. We had bought a small black-and-white cat, and May loved playing with Tinkle. Tinkle was a house cat, small and friendly and clean. We had lots of nice times with the cat, which was the first of many pets that were to invade my life and my heart.

Ever so quickly, Alex was back on board and off on his travels. My life went back to its usual routine. May was around seven months old and full of life. When I was on my own, my life was very busy. I did take to being a mum, and May and I had our own routine. There were no shops where we lived but a baker and a fish van. I walked to a nearby Council Estate, where there were shops. During this time, my brother and Alice and John left West Ferry to live outside Edinburgh. I still had my mum and dad, and my mum just loved hanging out the washing and making tea for dad and me. When I look back at that time, it is hard to believe they were the same parents as the ones I had just two years before. As spring went into summer, I was once again pushing the pram down to the station and home again up the steep brae in the evening. May, all this time, was thriving. She was by her first birthday the apple of everyone's eyes and was spoilt by both sets of grandparents. For her first birthday, I had a friend, who was a photographer, take pictures of her. I gave a number of them out to grannies, grandpas, uncles, aunts, friends, and, of course, the best to Daddy. Alex's brother had married Linda by this time. I was lucky my slim figure came back very quickly after the birth and I had great health. Life went on quietly; I so enjoyed being a mum—the excitement of May's first steps, then her little voice saying single words then small sentences. I had good neighbours and met other young wives for coffee. I still had my two best friends, Helen and Isabel. Isabel was married when May was still a baby, and she and Neil had moved into a house in the next street. Helen met James around this time. I had given up my Guiding in 1962, when I moved into my house in West Ferry. However, I remained involved as the Brownies Badge Secretary for Dundee Guide Association, and on Saturday mornings, I often got visits from Brownie Guiders wishing to buy badges but mostly it was done through the post.

I fed May for eight to nine months, gradually weaning her on to baby food and eventually giving her the same food as I ate but, of course, all mashed down. I had found a lump behind my ear some time before she was born, but I could get nothing done about it until May was weaned. I got an appointment for the ear, nose, and throat specialist at Dundee Royal Infirmary, and he arranged for it to be removed. May was to go to Granny and Papa Morays to stay, and they were absolutely thrilled, as you can imagine, to look after her. I even had a card from her telling me she had been a good girl and Granny and Papa were having a lovely time. There is a nice side to everyone. My lump was a benign tumour in my carotid gland, and I soon recovered, being cosseted by my mum.

Chapter 9

Another World Opens Up

By the time Alex came home, May was thirteen months old, and she walked to the door to meet this big man called Daddy. He decided that he did not want to stay at sea. He wanted to find a job at home so we could be a family. I was in a bit of a state about this as I knew that I would be blamed for him giving up the sea. I tried to explain this to him, but he said it was his decision. Before leaving the tanker for his leave, he had spoken to the Chief Engineer and told him he wanted to resign and leave the company. He, in turn, had told the captain; he, in turn, then passed on the information to their head office in London, and so before Alex left the ship, unbeknown to him, things were moving. He applied for a few jobs as he didn't want to leave the company until he had another position. However, a letter arrived to say that a position on the tugs in Abadan, South Iran, was his if he was interested. The job would be for a six-month trial; then he would be given leave, and if all went to plan, he would be able to arrange for his wife and daughter to join him. A house would be supplied for our use etc. We were thrilled; the pay was double of what he had been getting at sea and we would be able to live as a family. The icing on the cake was my being pregnant again. The baby was due in July 1965, and he ought to be home on leave at that time. We would all go out together or at least I would follow as soon as possible, but all would be arranged when he was still in Scotland.

We were in seventh heaven during that leave as he got himself prepared to have a shore job. He had all his injections, and we visited all our family and friends and had a party, and all too quickly, May and I waved him off on his new adventure.

The next few months went along quite smoothly in the usual fashion. My pregnancy went well, and I kept very well. Although I was looking forward to the birth, I had a bit of anxiety after the last time. May was thriving and was a lovely little girl. Just about a month before the baby was due, she became ill with a temperature and was proper poorly and had a bad cough. So I phoned my doctor. He said that there was measles in West Ferry, quite an epidemic, so that was what she had. I told him she had no spots.

'Well,' said he, 'she was breastfed for so long that she will have a high immunity to diseases. Hence no spots!' He arranged an antibiotic for her, and as the surgery was not far from my mum and dad's home, mum went for it. She took it to her local chemist, who happened to be a fellow bridge player and bowler, where she signed for it and Dad and she brought it down. May recovered from the cough and was as bright as a button again in no time. I had stopped walking down to the station and back, so Alex's mum came to visit more often. My mum and dad came to stay the week the baby was due to look after May and to keep an eye on me. I went into labour late in the evening after watching wrestling on the television. I don't know why I was watching wrestling as I didn't like it, but I think I was so restless and couldn't sleep and it was all that was on. I got my dad out of bed just after midnight on 8 July 1965, and he drove me to the hospital. This time I had no bother; it was all over by early morning. Margaret Elizabeth, weighing in at 8lb 3oz, our name choice for a girl. Once I was back in the ward, I expected to get her with me, but she did not arrive. I was then told that she was full of mucus and they had to clear her lungs before bringing her to me. She arrived beside me just before the evening visit of my dad. I was in for a few days, and I had my share of visitors; however, there was nothing from Alex. No message, no flowers—so different from the last time. Margaret was fair and had large blue eyes and a definite nose, her dad's nose. By the time I got home, I still hadn't any news—no flowers, no ship-to-shore message, nothing from Alex. I thought it was probably because he was coming home very soon, but I was disappointed. No one was showing the excitement that had been part of May's birth. So much so, that one day in the hospital, when I was feeding her I made her a promise that no matter what, she would be *my* precious special little girl. I went home to a busy time with a toddler and a new baby. My mum and dad stayed with me until Alex arrived some two weeks later.

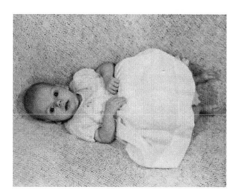

May aged 6 weeks

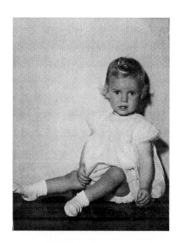

May aged 1 year

Margaret's christening, godmother holding
Margaret, May and mummy 1965

Godmother & Husband with
Margaret 1965

In garden in West Ferry with daddy.
prior to leaving for Iran 1965

Chapter 10

The Beginning—July 1965

He was full of life in Abadan and what he had been doing. We were not going to live in Abadan; we were going to Bandar Mashar, some seventy-eight kilometres from Abadan over the desert. It was a small place, but he said I would enjoy it as everyone was very nice. He had been to see the house and had met some of the other tug staff. He brought home the cork of the champagne bottle with which he had celebrated Margaret's birth! I didn't know what it was, but to me he had changed. I couldn't put my finger on it, but he appeared not to be so interested in being at home but wanted to go out and about. He started going out with Bill, our neighbour on Saturdays at lunchtime for a drink and wasn't so good at doing things around the house, even though we had a new baby and a little girl who needed his attention. I didn't know if I was feeling upset that he had not sent me his love and congratulations on the birth of Margaret. I wasn't worried about it being another girl, and he didn't seem to care one way or the other. There was plenty of time for us to have a son. I think I felt for the first time that he had let me down in some way. It may have been one of the reasons that I was so upset by what happened next.

We decided to have Margaret christened when she was six weeks old. We were having a lunch party in the afternoon for a few best friends and family. Ten persons, so I borrowed chairs from my neighbour, who was so good at helping me when or if I needed her. On Saturday morning, before he went for his 'pint' as he called it, I asked him to get the vegetables for the next day. I had bought everything else, just needed the fresh vegetables. Off he went and I was kept busy with Margaret and May. When he arrived home, he had not bought the vegetables, and for the first time in our married life we had a real argument. I suppose that somewhere I was hurt at his lack of interest in life in Scotland, and it seemed to me that he was taking me for granted. 'Margaret can manage!' I remember shouting that at him when Bill went out for his drink on a Saturday morning when he was off duty (he was a policeman); before he went, he had swept the rugs, washed the windows, hung out a washing, or worked in his garden. All he did was get up and have his breakfast, dress, and go off. When I asked him to give May her breakfast or dress her or clear the table, he either said he would do it later or did it with bad grace. I can remember him saying that he wasn't going to be henpecked by any woman and more on that line. I spent the afternoon between the girls and setting the table etc. for the next day so that when I came home from the church, everything would be ready but the 'vegetables'. He spent the afternoon in the garden cutting the grass etc. We never spoke then or all evening or even the next day. We went off to the christening; Isabel, who was her godmother, and Neil came for us, and we visited her mum and dad on the way to let them see Margaret dressed in her robe. Margaret was also christened in my father's family robe as May had been. On the way home Alex, went in and bought the vegetables, and his dad helped me to prepare them and get them on to cook immediately we got home. I didn't need to worry about the girls; they had plenty of friends to play with them. I fed Margaret, and she went off to sleep. Then we had our meal and photographs were taken. Strangely, when the photographs were developed, there was not one of me or Alex with Margaret. In fact, the only one I had of Margaret was taken with his mum, dad, and May on the front lawn of the house. I think that tells you something about the atmosphere between us. The grandparents went home after we had a late-afternoon tea. Margaret had been bathed and fed and bedded and May was ready for bed. The pair of us had acted as normal as we could all day, and by the time everyone left, we were halfway to being our usual selves again.

A few days after Margaret's christening, she appeared to be taking a cold. She was being fed by me and was very slowly putting on weight. I was feeding her on demand as she took a little but often, and being my second time, I was not so worried about routines; I had never done anything by the book. It suited our lifestyle to take Margaret into bed in the morning and feed her; then I would get up and wash and dress her and give her a top up. Then I would see to May before all three of us had our breakfast. We decided that Alex would go back to Iran first and we would join him, but before he went, we would take all our injections and the date, but would leave that until nearer the end of his leave. I loved my little family, and even before Alex had come home, I had done the journey to visit his mum and dad. I bought a seat for the high pram that May sat in and off I went. I have to say we only made the journey once after Alex returned as he just said it was too much.

I don't remember when I actually began to be a bit worried about Margaret. She wasn't putting on weight as I wanted. Then she started to be sick after her meals, and I put it down to her wee cold which she just never got rid of. Then the sickness became projectile, and I seemed to be spending most of my time feeding her. By evening my milk was beginning to dry up and by morning I could have fed all the babies in the street and beyond. I tried expressing in to a bottle and keeping it to feed her in the evening to give me a wee break. However, that didn't work, so I bought MSA baby milk, and this allowed Alex to feed her while he watched TV. My life seemed to be a never-ending cycle of feeding, washing clothes, and bedding, and somehow coping with May and Alex. They had to be fed and watered as well. When I asked the visiting Brown Nurse about her, all the support I got was being told 'feed her every two hours'. To be honest, she was more interested in our life than in Margaret. In the end, I went to the doctor and said I wanted to stop feeding her. The doctor wasn't very helpful. He was the same one who said I was pregnant when I wasn't and said May had the measles without spots. He wasn't interested in the fact that she was being sick all the time and that I was very worried about that and that was the reason I wanted to bottle-feed her. I could then judge how much she was getting. The feeding was happening night and day.

I was quite ill when my milk was drying up. It was a Saturday morning, and Alex and I were due that evening on a visit to his mum and dad's. He was going to a football match with Bill next door in the afternoon. After he left, my neighbour Ellen, who happened to be a nursing sister, came in to see how I was. I was in terrible pain. She bound me up and gave me a painkiller. She took May away to play with her wee girl and left me to sleep. She came in later on and took Margaret away and a made up bottle and fed her. She became aware then of how bad Margaret's sickness was. When Alex came in, he found me out for the count and was ashamed at having left me alone. I don't know to this day if Ellen had said something to him or not, but it was the last time he left me alone and he started to pull his weight in and around the house. In fact, he was more like my old Alex than he had been since he came home. With a two-year-old running about and Margaret not thriving as I wanted and being fed all the time, you can imagine how I was feeling. Sleep deprivation is a terrible thing. The sickness after every meal was no better, and Alex decided that we really had to do something about it. He had no faith in the nurse who visited; as I said, she was more interested in the paper we were putting on the wall than in what was happening to Margaret. In the end, he phoned the doctor and asked him to visit us. The doctor did this with bad grace, but he did come. By this time, I was beginning to be unable to cope with the workload. I only had an old-fashioned washing machine that I had to fill with a bucket and empty by a hose into a bucket. The washing was never-ending with a sick baby and nappies, plus May's clothes and Alex's, not to forget my own. The kitchen and dinette were like a Chinese laundry. It was worse on a rainy day. When the doctor came in, he really didn't want to be there. He said I was a 'fussing mother'. Alex asked him why he would think that I was a fussing mother when I didn't fuss over the first child, even though I was on my own with her for the first four months. Quite an argument took place, and Alex asked for another opinion. In the end, the doctor wrote a letter and handed it to Alex. He said, 'There is a paediatric clinic this afternoon in the DRI. Take this with you, seeing you are determined.' Alex told him he was due back in ten days' time and he couldn't leave me with two children, the way things were. Alex went off and phoned my dad to ask for his car. Dad, of course, said yes, and he went to Dundee to collect it from the car park Papa used. He came back and picked up May, Margaret, and myself. We took May to Granny and went off to Dundee Royal Infirmary (DRI). It was actually within walking distance of my mum and dad's house; although that day we had the car. We saw a paediatric doctor, who thought that Margaret had digestion trouble. He thought it could be allergic reaction to wheat or some other ingredient. When we left the hospital, we felt a weight had been lifted from our minds. Everything would be all right now. We visited every day, and every day they were still unable to find what was wrong with her. In the end, Alex had to leave and go back to Iran. When he left, the doctor told us that she probably had a hiatus hernia as they could find no result for any allergy.

Chapter 11

September-November 1965

At first, I travelled up to Dundee, taking two buses to my mum and dad's and left May with my mum; then I walked to the hospital and back, then travelled back home in the evening. As the doctors still puzzled over Margaret, it was decided that I should go to Mum and Dad's to stay for a while to give me a rest and not have to trail May out every day. It was by now the end of October, and Margaret had been in since the middle of September. Every day I went in she was sitting up in this little chair, neither getting bigger or smaller. She was very listless but still had a wee smile to give me. I very rarely got to feed her, and I was getting more and more worried as each day passed.

One day, a lovely baby was in the room next to Margaret's. When after days I never saw anyone visiting her, I asked the nurse, who I now knew very well, what was wrong with her. I was completely shocked when she said she had been abused and battered by her mother. The nurse told me that now they had put her together again she would probably go back to the mother, and in all probability, she would be back again. I cannot express in words my feelings. That lovely little baby, what I would have given to see my Margaret look like her. Fit and well and smiling, yet what a life she had had already. A part of me was so angry that any woman could be so cruel.

October moved into November, and Margaret was now on antibiotics as she had a chest infection, and they were putting her into an oxygen tent to help her breathing. I had not been home for weeks. I still never thought that she wouldn't get better; after all, she was in the best place. Then one Saturday, at the end of November, after ten weeks in hospital, the paediatric doctor called me into his office. It just happened that on that Saturday I had taken May in to see Margaret. She was enjoying herself staying with me at Granny and Papa's and was now two years and three months old. She was a great talker and a joy to all. She went skipping up to the wee room Margaret was in to speak to the nurses while

I spoke to the specialist. He had asked a paediatric specialist from Aberdeen Children's Department to come and see Margaret. She had done tests on her, and the results had come through. Margaret had fibrocystic disease of the pancreas. I had never heard of this disease so knew nothing whatsoever about it. I was then given a very big shock as her prognosis was nil. There was no cure, and she was extremely ill. She had pneumonia, and I had to prepare myself for the worst. However, as May skipped into the room with one of the nurses, the doctor looked at her and said, 'Well, she is OK anyway.' I walked slowly, pushing the pushchair up the hill back to my mum's in a shock. I could not believe it. I didn't even ask what the illness was. That was the first time I felt an empty pain in my chest. My first thought was to get Alex home, but as it was Saturday, I could do nothing until Monday. My dad took me back to hospital on Saturday night. I wasn't even able to hold her, and her breathing was extremely laboured. I went back again after breakfast on Sunday and sat with her, and they let me hold her just for a minute as she was in her oxygen tent. This time I was on my own, and I did not have to hold back my emotions. My special lovely little baby, that I had promised would be mine, was fighting for her life with no hope of being better. To say I was broken-hearted is just not the right word to describe my feelings; I was devastated. Before I walked home for my lunch, I told the nurses I would be back straight after and that I would be gone about one hour. I had just got in the door when the phone rang. My dad answered it. It was the hospital asking for me. The doctor told me Margaret had passed away just after I left and that it was peaceful. Because of her age and it being a sudden death, they would need to do an autopsy on her. This meant they would not release her body until probably Tuesday or Wednesday. They asked me to phone with the name of the funeral undertaker when I had managed to organise things. From then on, my mind was numb. I knew she was at peace, but my heart was broken. How do I describe in words what I felt to lose a child, a baby, five months old? I felt empty inside, and it hurt to breathe. You want to weep, but that doesn't help. All of that and much more I was feeling. You are not meant to lose your children; they are meant to grow and thrive and have a life and live on after you have gone. I can tell you in all honesty that you may get used to living with the grief as the years pass, but it never leaves you. There was no counselling in those days; you just had to get through as best you could.

Once we had all gathered our thoughts, my dad phoned Alex's mum and dad. I don't know what he said to them or what they replied. He then contacted our minister, who had married us and christened both May and Margaret. Then Dad contacted the undertaker, Mr Sturrock, who just happened to live at the end of their terrace and was a long-standing neighbour. There was nothing more we could do until the body was released, and so it was decided that we would all go back to West Ferry and do everything from there. I honestly don't remember very much about the next few weeks. I think I went into automatic mode. I did everything as usual on the outside, but I was dead on the inside. I remember very little, but a few things have stuck in my mind, like having to decide what to put in the papers. Of course I couldn't do that until I knew when her funeral was to be. I remember my dad contacted the oil company on Monday morning and was told they would get Alex home as soon as possible, but being Iran, he would have to get an exit visa etc., so they couldn't be sure how long it would take. I kept hoping I would hear from him or the company, but the days seemed to me to be a blur. The funeral was all arranged and the notice was placed in the papers. The cards poured into the house; I never knew until then how many friends we had. I can't remember if I saw my in-laws at all, but they must have visited. I will never forget her small white coffin as Mr Sturrock brought her home to rest overnight. I never saw her after she died, I never said goodbye. I had asked and was told to remember her the way she was alive. Now I know that was a cruel thing. In the 1960s, there was no help or support for grieving mothers and dads; you just had to get on with it. I am sure that a lot of woman must have died of broken hearts. My mum and dad were there for me and saw to everything. They helped me with the music for the service and the flowers and the food for those coming back to the house after the service. In those days, you didn't go to hotels etc. You just had a nice afternoon tea and a sherry or something similar for those who wanted a wee drink. Still no word from Alex, I had given up hope of his getting home before the funeral. We had given the company time to get him home. I vaguely remember the minister in my house and the service there. My next recollection is walking down the centre of what seemed to me to be a huge crematorium in Dundee, but I know it is not as large as it seemed that day. I could not bear to watch her coffin going and I remember shutting my eyes and hoping I would stay in one piece until I got out of that place. On the way home, we dropped off the minister, and I remember him saying to me, 'Well, you married a sailor, and that is what that life is like'. I don't know why he said it. It must have been a conversation that my mum and dad were having with him about Alex not getting home. I always thought it a funny peculiar remark to make as I had never even said anything about Alex not being at home, not then or at any time in that terrible week.

A cable came the next day to say he was on his way, and the company contacted my dad at his work to say he was on his way home. I later found out that as usual, everything was in slow motion and it took days to get his exit visa and his passport back from the relevant office. I was to understand about these things later in my life. I don't remember anything about his homecoming. I think my mind and body had switched off. I do believe now that I was in shock, and my grief was so much that I was numb. I have been told by my friends and relatives since then that I was so brave!

Chapter 12

New Places, New Faces

One of the things I do remember was the visit to the paediatric doctor in DRI. Alex had made an appointment for us to see him after we received a letter from the hospital. He told us about fibrocystic disease of the pancreas, known now as cystic fibrosis. He told us how it was a genetic illness caused by both of us carrying a recessive gene which did not cause us any bother, but any children born to us had a one in four chance of being born with the disease. There was no cure, and the prognosis was not good. Very few babies lived to reach school age. The pancreas did not make digestive juices as normal but secreted, instead, sticky mucus which was prone to infection. The pancreas was also unable to digest the food properly, especially fats, and so it passed through the body in some cases without doing any good. He said a lot more, and, of course, we became interested in CF. Alex found out a little more for us at that time. You have to remember that it was 1965 and few doctors had ever seen patients with CF. However, the doctor never at any time asked if we wanted May tested for the disease. He had already said to me she didn't have it after seeing her running about the ward. Since that day, of course, we have learnt a great deal more about the illness and the treatment, from physiotherapy to diet and a lot more in between. Now in Scotland, babies are tested for this at birth. However, none of my family or Alex's had ever heard of this illness at that time. In fact, his mother said something which did penetrate my brain. She said, 'It wasn't in their side of the family and so had nothing to do with Alex!' Now these children with the proper treatment can live until they are in their thirties.

It changed our life completely; we had always wanted children, and we had not intended to stop at the two girls. Alex always teased me about the size of the families amongst the staff in Iran. He used to write and joke about there being no television. I always thought we would have a large family, well, not six but maybe four. We were in a comfortable position in life and had no money worries once he went to Iran. All that changed that memorable day. How could I morally bring into the world another child knowing that it could be born with a genetic disease that could kill it before it was five years old? To watch another child suffer as Margaret had was unthinkable in my mind. I knew from that day it was unlikely that I would give birth to any more babies. However, we had a lot of other things to think about.

Alex had two weeks' compassionate leave. He wanted May and me to travel back with him. He had already been on to the company and our flights were booked and visas would be arranged. May had to be put on my passport and we required such and such injections. The day after we visited the hospital, he went down to Dundee to see our solicitor regarding the looking after of the house, the paying of the mortgage, etc. However, when he came back, he had not only arranged to sell the house, but buyers were coming that afternoon. They would view the house at 5 p.m. I do not in all honesty remember them coming, but they bought the house. One day, the baker's van man asked me what I was going to do with the cat. I didn't know. However, he said his wife was a cat lover and she had said she would take it when he told her all about what was happening. So Tinkle went off to a new home.

My next real memory is emptying the house. May and I had just had our smallpox vaccination and other jags, and I can remember feeling really awful. I sat on a nursing chair in the kitchen while they pulled my home apart. Did I want to take this to Iran or did that go in to the store? I must have answered, but when it came time to empty it at the other end, I had absolutely no idea what I had packed. I think Alex managed most of it himself. I can't remember leaving West Ferry, or leaving Dundee. I can't remember saying goodbye to my mum and dad or Alex's parents or any of our friends. My mum and dad must have been heartbroken to see us go, and I can't tell you if they were or not. The trip to London is a blank; the hotel in London and the start of the plane journey to Beirut is a blank, yet I must have been acting normal. The body and mind do strange things, and maybe that was the only way I could have got through those weeks.

Chapter 13

Abadan, Iran, December 1965

Somewhere on the final leg of the journey between Beirut and Abadan by BOAC, I came to life. My first real memory is sitting on the plane with May between Alex and me. I had on the pink dress that I had bought for Margaret's christening, and my arm was very sore. The edge of the sleeve had been rubbing on the smallpox scab and had knocked it slightly, and it was bleeding. I was very hot and so was May. My arm was swollen and very red, and I was sure it had an infection in it. I often thought when trying to remember this time that the physical pain had become so bad that it penetrated my mind and brought me back to reality.

It was getting dark outside, and Alex was telling May and me to 'look outside and see the gas flares'. We were circling around Basra in Iraq, making our final turn before landing in Abadan. I had dreamt about this journey so many times over the past few months but never in the circumstance that we found ourselves in. Once the plane landed, May and I tried to see the buildings in the distance, but it was now quite dark all of a sudden. Then the door of the plane was opened, and my first experience of the difference between Scotland and Abadan happened.

Firstly, the heat—it was the beginning of December, but it so happened that it was a humid night. Secondly, it was the smell of Shatt Al-Arab, the river; although, I did not know that then. It hung in the air—the damp atmosphere and the smell. Alex carried May down the stairs from the plane, and I followed. I could make out the long low buildings with lots of lights. It felt quite cold once you were out in the evening air, yet the humidity hit me, making me feel that my clothes were sticking to my body. I followed along beside Alex carrying the bag with all our travel bits and pieces, wondering where I was going. Then we went through the double door of the Arrival and Customs part of Abadan airport building at that time. The noise was awful. People were shouting and jostling, pushing and shoving. I was frightened I would lose Alex in the melee. All the people were speaking and shouting in a language I had never heard before—porters, policemen, soldiers with guns! Women were all dressed in black or grey printed cloaks (chadors) that covered them completely. In some cases, they even had their faces covered in a mask. There were other women dressed in the height of fashion and were much more glamorous than I was. I was frightened, excited, and very apprehensive. Then we were at a counter, and Alex was handing over our passports and visas. I held my breath as they questioned everything; this man was in a white shirt and black trousers. Then after what seemed an age, he stamped everything and we were through. The next thing I knew, we were once again in a melee, trying to find our cases. May and I stayed still and let the people go round us. I cuddled her close to me, as I didn't want these people all smelling of some unusual thing being near her. Then the next thing was opening our cases and watching a dark swarthy man going through my clothes and May's clothes. Eventually, after what seemed like an age, we were allowed to close the cases and leave the building.

We left the custom hall and stepped through into Arrivals. I heard English voices shouting 'Hello, Alex', and I was clasped into a lady's arms. A gentleman was speaking away to Alex and saying how pleased he was to meet me, and they both gave me such a lovely, friendly welcome. I felt safe at last. Peter and Gill Sim, a tug captain and his wife, had a company car and driver waiting to take us to the Abadan Hotel for the night. I don't remember ever being so glad to get out of any place. The smell, the dirt, and the noise were overbearing, especially after a journey that had started at 11 a.m. in London and it was coming up for 9 p.m., Abadan time.

I wasn't able to see very much on the way from the airport to the hotel, but the road seemed very modern and I was greatly surprised when we turned into the hotel. It was large with glass windows along the front—very modern on the outside—and the inside very spacious. Once Alex had signed in, we were taken to our room. Alex invited Peter and Gill up to the room and they said they would come for a little while as we would want to settle in. I bathed May and had milk and bread and butter sent up for her. She had eaten everything she was given on the plane, but I wanted something for her to drink before going to bed. She wasn't very keen on the taste of the bread or the milk but took enough to satisfy me. I put her into the cot in the room, and she stood and watched us as Peter discussed what was to happen tomorrow and Gill said she would take me to a coffee morning while Alex was at the office. Once they left, May fell asleep, and we had a meal and a drink brought up. I was glad to have arrived and to be more like myself. I never asked Alex what happened to me in those weeks and he never told me anything, so I have always believed that I had acted as normally as one would be expected to under the circumstances.

The next morning, the three of us had breakfast together, and I couldn't get over the different people in the hotel. Lots of different languages were going on, but predominantly English; however, the accent was American. We sat in the lobby of the hotel, looking out the huge glass windows on to palm trees and flower beds. I noticed that the Iranian men were quite small compared with the Europeans and Americans. There were also Arabs in their long white robes and the headdresses just like in *Lawrence of Arabia*. Alex told me that they were from the other side of the Gulf, where alcoholic drink was prohibited, so they came to Iran for a holiday. Only the men came. It wasn't long before Gill came for me in a taxi, and Alex went off in the car that had been sent to collect him. I got on very well with Gill very quickly and always did. She was a tall slim woman, very dark in colouring. I always felt that she had coloured blood in her, but, of course, she had spent a number of years in Iran so I suppose she had a very nice tan on top of her dark colouring.

I have to say that I was not sure what to expect. Alex never said very much to me about what I would find when I lived in Iran. He said I was to wait and see as he didn't want to disappoint me by making me think it was wonderful or put me off by giving me the wrong impression. I was so surprised when, after travelling along the main road for a short time, we turned into a tree-lined road with pavements and deep ditches between them and the road. Each gate had a bridge of slabs to cross from the road to the pavement. It was like any housing estate of bungalows in the United Kingdom with gardens behind hedges, and I could see quite substantial houses as we passed the double gates. We drove into one of the gates and up to the front door of the house.

I was a bit nervous as this was my first contact with the people I would meet in my new life. When I walked into that room with its Persian carpets, its gold-framed pictures, and a grand piano in the corner, I was completely speechless. Gill took me up to a lady of ample proportions, who was sitting in a chair near a massive fireplace. She introduced me to the lady and this very English voice said the name of the oil company as a question.

'___?'
I said, 'Yes.'
'Welcome,' she said and dismissed me by talking to someone else. I often wonder what she would have said if I had said no to her question. Maybe I would have been shown the door. I sat in a corner with May and sipped my tea—I didn't want to try the coffee—and we had a biscuit. May had a drink of orange juice, and I remember her wee face was a picture as she watched

all these 'ladies' talking to each other about things we knew nothing about. At last a houseboy came and said that a car was waiting for me. Gill came and said goodbye, and I thanked her for her kindness. She said she would no doubt see me again when I came to Abadan. I slipped quietly out of the room, and I am sure no one even noticed. The car took May and me back to the hotel, where we had some lunch. The tea had an awful taste just like the tea I had at breakfast and the coffee morning. I realised it was the milk. It was powdered milk; good for you but to me it was horrible. The bread wasn't very nice either, but May and I ate the ham and the tomatoes. 'Ham', I hear you say, 'in a Muslim country?' Well, that's the way it was in Iran in 1965. Then it was time to go to the room and collect all our bits and pieces and make ourselves comfortable as we had a long journey in front of us, over the desert.

Chapter 14

Bander Mashar, December 1965

When I saw the car, I thought it would never get us anywhere. We left the hotel and to begin with we went past some blocks of flats, then shops and the houses. We seemed to be driving along the side of the estate I had been in that morning. Alex informed me, as we were travelling along, that the flats on the right were where the bachelors and the single ladies lived. The shop was the IPA book and paper shop and the houses on the left that I had visited that morning were Braim housing area. When I told him about our visit, he didn't know who the woman was, but he said she must have been the wife of one of the office bosses who worked in the oil refinery.

Then I got my first sight of the other side of Iran. We travelled along through a row of shops, just shacks made of odd bits of wood and cardboard. Some had corrugated roofs and sides and some had bits of cloth as sides. All had open fronts, and all the goods were outside. All of life could be seen, from live hens to food and pots and tins—just a dirty mess. Little children were playing in the dust, dressed in rags, and had dirty faces. I couldn't help but look aghast after the house I had been in, in the morning. 'Poverty amongst the oil rich' is what it seemed to be to me. The rest of the journey was taken up trying to keep May amused and giving her plenty of drinks and biscuits and reading stories as there was nothing to see out of the window but a pipeline. The road had disappeared quite a while ago, and we were driving on desert sand with a few scrub patches following the pipeline. Then quite suddenly, the car veered off to the right and left the pipeline behind. My mind was in a turmoil. How did the driver know where he was going?

Then Alex said, 'Can you see the top of the mosque, the minarets, where the mullah calls the people to prayers? That is Bandar Masher.' Vaguely, at first I saw the tops of buildings, and then a jumble of buildings came into sight. We travelled until we got on to a road which had buildings along it, but I couldn't be sure if they were houses. Then we came to a part with semi-detached bungalows, a street similar to the one I had been in earlier in the day but with much smaller houses and the hedges a bit straggly. We turned a corner, and Alex told May that she would soon be in her new home. We drew up at a gate, and standing outside were Shona and John Macintosh, whom I had met two years before on board the tanker at Grangemouth, with their three children—two girls, whom I knew about, and a toddler, a boy named John. I know I was in a bit of a daze, but it was nice to see someone I knew. They had tea ready for us, so we did not linger in our new home. Alex had bought me a Pointer puppy, a big gangly animal with liver and white colouring, which he had called Tojo, after a dog he had become friendly with in Abadan belonging to one of the engineers. After a welcome from him, a surprise I have to say, and a quick look around and a wash and a brush, we went around to Shona and John's, who lived in the other half of the semi. We had a nice time with them, with lots of laughter as both the girls were as bright as buttons and full of all the things they were doing.

When we got back to the house, I had a good look at my new home. I ought to tell you what it looked like. You walked into a closed-in veranda, then into a large room with a lounge area on the left and dining area on the right. All the furniture was company furniture with mustard-coloured suite and wooden arms and legs. There was a wood-veneered dining table, eight dining chairs, and mustard seats—of course. The bureau, coffee table, desk, and side tables, all had the same shiny veneer. Shona and Johns' was just the same; in fact, everyone had the same furniture, though, if my memory isn't playing tricks, some had green seats and cushions. Alex had bought or been given a carpet of sorts for the tiled floor. There were two bedrooms and a bathroom off to the left through a door. Once again the furniture was the same style—chest of drawers, two single beds in each room, bedside cabinets, and a dressing table. The bathroom was basic but clean. The kitchen was off the dining area of the main room. There was a large fridge, enormous to my eyes, on the wall just to the right of the door as you walked into the kitchen. I must say something about the fridge. For one thing, I had never owned one so that was to be a new experience. However, it was the inside that caused me the biggest puzzle or even consternation. When I looked into it that first day, I was met with a row of bottles. There were bottles of vodka, whisky, and wine, in fact, as I found out any sprit bottle did. However, it wasn't spirit in them but water which had been filtered for drinking. The kitchen was quite spacious, compared to the one in Scotland, with units on one side and a sink and cooker on the other.

There was a large cupboard, then an area where the houseboy slept, then another deep sink at the back door for the purpose of washing clothes. It was very bare with dull colours; in fact, I don't think I could tell you any of the colours in that house. The windows were quite large, however; one looked into the veranda and all had mesh screens, so the whole house was rather dark. It did not take us long to get to bed that night, and even with all the excitement, we all slept soundly.

Chapter 15

Life as I Had Never Known It

I began to find out more about Alex's job and the oil companies that ran the industry. I knew that Abadan had the largest oil refinery at that time, anywhere. I also knew that it had jetties for the oil tankers on the Shatt Al-Arab as Alex had been there with the oil tankers when at sea. I also knew that Bandar Mashar was also a 'tanker port' and that he had been there also. Alex's job was working as an engineer on the tugs that berthed these oil tankers. John was one of the captains. There was a captain and an engineer plus an Indian crew on the tugs at Bandar Masher. There was also an island, Kharg Island, in the Persian Gulf which was being developed but was in its infancy at that time. The men ran a shift system so Alex could be on the tug for twenty-four hours then on standby for the next, and then off the next.

I met the expatriates a few at a time; Shona took me to the badminton courts, and a few of the young wives were there. I have to say that there was not a lot of badminton being played that morning. There were a lot of arguments about the rules by one of the women. She was a Welsh woman, who seemed to know everything. One of the women, a dark, pretty person, Mary, was another Scot. She came from Arbroath and was the wife of the shipping agent. It so happened that I knew about the family she was married into. My first job was in the Timber Merchants who did business with a company in Arbroath; her husband, Paul, was a younger son of this family. I never went back to the badminton courts. I couldn't be bothered with all the nonsense. My mind was still trying to recover from what had happened to us. I had enough on my plate with getting used to the new surroundings and having a houseboy, shopping in the Staff Store, and meeting different people. Most of the expatriates were very kind and asked me round in the mornings for coffee. Sometimes they were planned, but more often than not, there was just a phone call, 'Come round, a few of us have got together'. One house in particular always had some of the young wives visiting. Gertie was an Irish lady of middle years and was a cheery person. She loved all the visitors, and it was always a happy atmosphere in her house. If you did not make your own enjoyment, there was very little to do. There were badminton and tennis courts, along with a golf course and a cinema, at the Mashar Club. There was an American Seamen's Club for the sailors from the oil tankers from where they could buy personal things that were on sale, when they came ashore. They could have a drink and something to eat.

Thursday nights were the main entertainment nights at the Golf Club—the hub of the expats' social life. The first Thursday night (the equivalent to Saturday in United Kingdom) that we went along to the Golf Club, I remember well. As we were getting ready, Alex told me that most of the expats would be there.

'Now', he said, 'remember that you can't get rum out here. The only spirit we can get is vodka as they make it here in Iran.' My drink, when on an occasional night out at home, was a Bacardi rum and Coke. 'Whisky', he said, 'we keep for our houses, when we can get it off the ships. Beer they make in Iran, so there is always plenty of it. Just don't ask for rum.'

Why, oh why did he say that to me? I was nervous as it was. I was leaving May with the houseboy, Caliph, for the first time, and I was to meet most of the people from the oil company and the shipping agents etc. who lived in Mashar. When we got there, I was introduced to Fred Richards; he was from Aberdeen and was one of the engineers. He looked after the social side of the Golf Club. He immediately asked me what I would like to drink.

'Vodka and rum,' I said.

He shouted, 'We have one of us here! She wants a vodka-rum!'

I could have curled up and died with embarrassment. That first evening there was a whist drive. I had never played whist, so I got the booby prize; in fact, the two times I went, I got the booby prize. The second time, it was a monkey you wound up and he turned somersaults. It had a card on it which said, 'This monkey can turn somersaults, but you can't play whist'. Very true. I didn't get off to a very auspicious start. However, I think I really did myself a good turn as I very quickly fitted in.

The houseboy was a young man who had worked for an Aberdeen couple before they moved to Kharg Island.

He was able to make mince and potatoes and tomato soup but little else. I had no idea how to treat a servant. I had never had any experience with one except the 'boy' who had looked after Alex, when I visited him in South Shields prior to our marriage. When I was in the kitchen making the food, he usually took off to the shops for me. When he was cooking, he had a habit of putting his head round the door and saying, 'Lunch in fifteen minutes'.

One day, the phone rang and the Welsh girl said, 'Come over for coffee.'
I replied, 'I can't. I am about to have lunch.'
'Lunch?' she said 'It is only 11.30.'
'But it is made,' I replied.
'Well, tell him to keep it hot and come right over. You're the boss, not him.'

I sheepishly went into the kitchen and told Caliph I was going out and to turn off the soup and he could reheat it when I got back. Then I took off as quickly as I could with May in tow. May seemed to be settling all right. She was a bit quiet but was sleeping well. The food was a difficulty. Not the main meals of the day but the bread, milk, eggs, and butter all had distinctive tastes and smells, not like home. She was a bit shy with all the people and kept very close to me when we were out and about.

I was beginning to get into the life. I had the usual everyday things to do—my shopping, washing and looking after May. Caliph did all the housework, and I started showing him how to make the things we liked, if and when they were available so he did more and more of the cooking. Thursday nights and the curry lunch on a Friday at the Golf Club were the main entertainments. There was an outdoor cinema, but I don't remember being at it very often. Life was very much contained within the expatriate community. This was really the tug staff and a few contractors and the shipping agents. I can't remember any other people, although there must have been more. I knew my next-door neighbour on the other side from Shona and John was an Iranian ship's pilot; I don't even remember speaking to them or seeing them anywhere until years later.

The weather in December and January was pleasant, more like spring in Scotland; it was not to remain like that, and I was going to find out later how the summer in Iran on the Persian Gulf coast could become.

It was the run-up to Christmas and the New Year. It seemed to be the talking point. Fred Richards was organising a dance for Hogmanay, and the ladies were asked to come to the Golf Club to see about the food for the night.

I met the teacher from the school. There was only one teacher as the children went home when they were nine years to be educated. The ladies present all seemed to know what they would contribute to the meal. When the list was ticked off, the only things left were potato salad and coleslaw. The teacher chose potato salad, and I was left to make the coleslaw. I went home to Alex to find out what it was. He told me that I had the makings of it in the fridge. There I was, door open, calling out one by one what was on the shelves. When I said, 'Cabbage', he said 'yes'; when I said 'carrot', he said 'yes'; when I said 'Mayonnaise', he said 'yes'. That was my introduction to coleslaw. I managed to make mostly everything we liked to eat as a family, availability being the prime difficulty, except for bread. My first and last attempt at making rolls at that time came out looking and weighing like golf balls; even the dog was beat to eat them.

Christmas day was for the children. We had brought out May's presents (I can't remember buying them, but quite a lot was from family) and had managed to get one or two extras in the only shop in Mashar. After May had opened her presents from Santa, we exchanged gifts, had breakfast, and dressed. Then we went down to the tugboat Alex worked on and had drinks before being served a lovely Christmas meal. We had turkey with all the trimmings and Christmas pudding—the lot. Then we went home for a siesta. In the late afternoon, we went to the Seaman's Club for a children's party. They had a Christmas tree, balloons, and a gift for all the children from Santa Claus. It was a very happy time, although by evening, May was weepy, but she had had a busy day.

Very soon it was Hogmanay and the dance in the Golf Club. In fact, life was all dances at that time, as I remember, in the Mashar Club and during New Year as well. My wardrobe was depleted as I just hadn't taken out enough clothes. My present from Alex was a sewing machine. It was an all-singing, all-dancing machine, state of the art. I was very glad to get it and was able to get material in the bazaar to make myself some suitable dresses for all the parties.

Once all the festivities were over, I felt just a bit down. I don't think my feet had touched the floor since my arrival, and because of that I had had no time to think or look back. May had caught a cold somewhere and was a bit off-colour. I decided to take her to see the doctor in the clinic in Mashar, a Dr Sami. She had a chest infection and was put on the antibiotic Terramycin. She seemed to get better and was very quickly her old self, except her tummy was upset. I thought it might be the antibiotic or the change of food. May and I were finding the food a difficulty as I could not get her the things she had liked at home. It took me a while to find a cereal she liked, and the powdered milk wasn't to her taste or mine. She seemed to be thriving all the same, and I wasn't worried as we had only been out for five weeks. However, not long after she had recovered from the chest infection, I saw no improvement in her tummy upset, and then she took another chest infection. She really was very poorly this time, and I nursed her very carefully. I began to have a terrible thought. When the doctor said she had pneumonia, I really began to have loud alarm bells in my head of enormous proportions. This time she wasn't getting better as quickly as she had the last time, and she had the cough she had when we were at home, the time the doctor said she had measles without spots! I tried to sort things out in my mind. Was I worrying for nothing? Was I letting my imagination run away? I kept coming back to the same conclusion—the infection in her chest combined as it was with the cough and the bowel trouble. My other concern was Alex; I did not want to upset him for nothing. It was the hardest thing I ever had to do in my life. If my thoughts were correct, I was about to shatter our lives. He was so happy having May and me with him. I was beginning to understand why he seemed so different when he came home after Margaret's birth. Life here was free from the chains of the restrictions of living life as our parents lived. We were living life to the full. Alex worked in conditions that were less than good, but when he was off duty, we had lots of fun, laughter, and play. I was so miserable inside, so frightened of the future that I decided I just had to speak to Alex about it. That night, I told him what was in my mind—that I was pretty sure May had fibrocystic disease of the pancreas, or cystic fibrosis. I could not believe it when he told me that he also had the same thoughts. We decided that the next day he would go and speak to Dr Sami and explain to him the situation. Then we would get her home. I was so calm on the outside but terrified inside. It couldn't happen to us again, could it? Yes, it could, I knew she had all the symptoms—the loose bulky bowel motion, the chest infection, the cough, and worse, the breathlessness. She had also begun to lose weight quickly. Dr Sami arranged for her to go up to the hospital in Aga Jari. It was a small place an oil well town, up on the plateau some seventy or eighty miles away. Once all the arrangements were made, I packed a case for myself and May as I did not know how long I would be away. The arrangements were made very quickly, and before I knew it, May and I were on our way in a car.

House in Bander Mashar, Iran

House in Bander Mashar, Iran

May with daddy, Christmas 1965-Iran

May with mummy, Christmas 1965—Iran

May, Nurse and mummy, Hospital garden,
Abadan, June 1966

May with mummy, |Hospital garden,
Abadan, June 1966

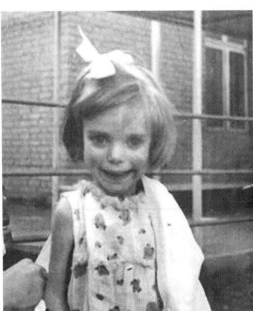

May on her own, Hospital garden,
Abadan, June 1966

May with Nurse, Hospital garden,
Abadan, June 1966

Chapter 16

Nightmare Journeys, January 1966

This journey is one that I will never forget for more than one reason. At the start of the journey, we travelled across the flat desert towards the mountains. Iran on the west end of the Persian Gulf coast around Bander Mashar was made up of mudflats and desert. Once you travel inland for a varying number of miles, you come to the escarpment of the plateau that makes up the vast area of Iran. The road I had to travel on was a winding, twisting, corkscrew road up the side of the escarpment on to the plateau. Luckily as far as the journey went, May was no bother; she just wanted to lie and sleep, wrapped in her favourite blanket. Although she was breathless, she was free of the cough during the journey. The only thing I can remember seeing on the desert part of the journey was passing a building and an airstrip sitting all on its own in the desert. After that, we drove on a proper road, and not long after that, we reached the winding road that was to take me on a hair-raising ride up the mountain to the plateau above. Later in my life, I was to journey through the Sierra Nevada Mountains of California. The difference then was the road itself. In America, although I was travelling at higher altitudes, it was a modern two-lane, well-made and finished road. It had double barrier at the cliff edge of the road and another double barrier at the sheer cliff side. There was nothing like that on the roads in 1966 Iran. As the car travelled on the right side of the road, going left one way, I had a sheer cliff rising straight up out of the window. I could have touched it if I had felt like it. Then worse, as the road wound, we turned right at a hairpin bend, I had a sheer drop down the side of the mountain and could see the road we were on far below. No barrier. I was petrified. If you have ever been to a Middle Eastern country, then you will know how they drive. The Highway Code doesn't exist. They drive anywhere they like on the road, usually with their hand on the horn. By the time we reached the flat land on the top, I was feeling very, very sick. May, thank goodness, had slept through it.

Then the next shock—the hospital was, as I remember, a few low buildings. I have to admit I paid very little attention to the surroundings as my mind was very taken up with the idea that I was out on my own here. I had to try to get help for May, but what they could do here was limited. I was correct. They had no oxygen tent, so they put a sheet over the cot and stuck the oxygen straight into the space at one end by means of a plastic tube and, at the other end, a steam kettle. I could speak no Farsi; they could speak no English. They dealt with injuries and illnesses of the drillers at the wells. Anything remotely difficult and they transferred their patients to MIS, the largest of these towns, up in the mountains. They put up a bed for me in May's room while they thought what to do with her. She must have been restless when I went to have something at the canteen, and when I came back, she had burnt her foot on the kettle. This was just one more thing to worry about. I was really desperate; all I had wanted was to fly her to London. Remember please that in a Muslim country, the women have no say in family matters, especially dealing with matters out with the home. So I had to wait to see what Alex and Captain Blair, the boss in Bander Mashar, would decide with the doctors. At last, I heard I was to fly to Abadan. It was decided that as Alex and I knew no one in MIS, it was better for me to go to Abadan Hospital where I could get help and support from friends. After two days in Agi Jari, we were off on our travels again.

I learnt that to get to the airfield, I had to go down that awful road again. My heart was in my mouth, and May, who by now was a poor wee soul, was very breathless and coughing and had a sore burn on her foot to make matters worse. I had her all wrapped up against the cold of the mountains in my arms, and off we went. If I was afraid on the way up, I have no words that would even touch on how I felt on the way down. It was a never-ending journey; every time we passed a lorry or car going in the opposite direction, I felt I was either going to be crushed against the cliff wall or be pushed over the side of the mountain. At last, we arrived at the buildings and the airstrip that I had seen on my way to Aga Jari. The plane to Abadan had not yet arrived, so we had to wait in the 'Waiting Room'! When we arrived, a young man was sitting, waiting, and he introduced himself to me. Andrew Simpson, he was the English church minister who lived in Ahwaz. He was on his monthly visit to the 'fields' which included Aga Jari, Bander Mashar, Kharg Island, and a service in Abadan's St Christopher Church. I told him what had happened, and he said that he would be in Mashar in a day or two and would hear how I was getting on from Alex. His plane arrived to take him to Kharg Island, and mine arrived very shortly to take me to Abadan. I was just glad to get on with my journey. When we arrived in Abadan, a car was waiting to take me to the hospital.

I will never fault the treatment that May got in Abadan. She was too ill to travel by plane to the United Kingdom. The doctor in charge of the hospital, a Sri Lankan, was so kind. The paediatric doctor in charge was wonderful.

He was an Iranian, but I never did master his name. He had qualified in France. He had never treated any child with CF (I will call it that from now on). It did not stop him; they took X-rays of the lungs to see how badly they had been affected. They contacted Paris, where one of the young doctors in the department had also trained and knew someone who could help them. I was given a room with a couple, who lived in South Bawarda. The housing in Abadan was built around the refinery. Braim was built on the west side with North and South Bawarda on the east. He was a captain on the tugs. They were very kind, and all my washing and ironing was done for me. The only thing was they both liked a drink. Now in Iran, most of the expatriates liked a drink, some more than others. However, this couple's idea of a drink was an all-evening session. All I wanted was a bath, a drink, a meal, and then bed. I very quickly realised that it wasn't any good my staying there. Alex came through on Friday morning and spoke to the doctors. They had two aims—try and save her life, then get her to the United Kingdom. Alex realised that although it was fine for him, staying with the couple at the weekend, it was not for me when he was at work. They were very kind to me, and I did appreciate their help. I spoke to the sister on the ward and told her what it was like, and she spoke to matron a Miss Eloise Basswood, who was English, and the doctor in charge and it was decided that I would stay in the hospital. May's room was fitted up with a bed for me and a chair and a table. It already had a separate shower, toilet, and wash basin. I would go and stay at the couple's when Alex came to Abadan. This way, we did not have to hurt anyone's feelings as Alex told them that the hospital had suggested this. Their boy kindly did my washing and ironing, and I always paid him when I stayed there on Friday nights.

Chapter 17

Abadan Hospital: January to July 1966

By this time, May was being fed fluids through a tube in her nose. She had a needle permanently in her hand to feed all the antibiotics. Her breathing was much laboured, but she had no cough! She looked like the children on a poster for famine relief. Her legs and arms were pin thin, but the joints stood out. Her tummy was all swollen. Her eyelids drooped, and her face was tiny. She was very still, but she could still smile. Yet somehow it never entered my head that she might die. I got into a routine, staying at the hospital. My life was very restricted, and my contact with the outside was practically nil. I was able to nurse May and help as much as I could. Even though she was disappearing before my eyes, she had that vital spark, and the nurses just loved her. The doctors had now amassed as much knowledge as they could. She was in an oxygen tent at night and on a concoction of antibiotics. They reduced the amount of fat in her diet as much as they could, and this did help her bowels. I knew from the start that it could be a battle that may not be won, but if I could get her to the United Kingdom, then I had faith that all would be well.

There were interesting moments which made me realise a bit more about life and people. One day I had a visit from the minister of St Christopher's Church, in Abadan, an American Presbyterian, although, if my memory isn't playing tricks, I could swear he sounded English. He was elderly in my eyes, and he gave me the impression that he was there because he had to come. He said a prayer and off he went. Not long after that, I had a visit from Father Milligan, the Catholic priest. His church was in Khorramashahr, the port a few miles up the Shatt Al-Arab from Abadan He was cheerful and bright and told May he had seen her daddy the night before, and he said he was sure he would have a sore head today. It was above May's head but not mine. That was when I realised that Alex was drinking rather a lot. It was confirmed when I asked him to start bringing me a bag of clothes when he came through to see us and he very rarely remembered. Sometimes he just forgot to bring them; sometimes, when he came, he would bring me books to read, and I knew he had bought them in the bookshop in Abadan before getting a taxi to the hospital. I wasn't in a position to do anything about it, and it was no use worrying about it. It was obviously his way of coping with the terrible situation we were in. He was such a gentleman, and I loved him and he loved me and that was enough for the moment. To get back to Father Milligan, he said he would try and come in every day and if I required anything, I was to write it down. If he could not buy anything for me, he would get the sisters to buy it. He was my lifeline to the outside world. He was able to buy my digestive biscuits, crisps, Coke, soap, toothpaste, in fact all my personal needs. He remained a friend until the end of my time in Abadan years later. The matron, as I said, was English, and she was quite a character. I was not to find out how much of a character she was until some years later. She was one of father's parishioners, so I expect that is how he heard about me.

Another significant time was months later; the doctors had been telling father that they required more antibiotics for May and they wondered if he had any pull with the oil company, especially the one Alex worked for, to try to get more. Father went to Captain Rogers, the superintendent and boss of the tugs to see if he could help. I did not know anything about this until father came in absolutely fizzing.

'Can you believe what Captain Rogers said? Is she one of yours?'

Captain Rogers was a member of the Presbyterian St Christopher Church, an elder, etc. 'I just told him', said father, 'it doesn't matter if she is or not. She is a very sick child who is in need of our help. They are running out of antibiotics that she requires in the hospital, and, by the way, she is not.'

That led to a very unforgettable day in my life. After a lot of discussion somewhere it was decided that the drugs would be flown in as they were desperately required for May. Alex and I couldn't do it; we couldn't get them off the NHS, nor could any of our families. I found myself at the airport building one evening quite late, waiting for the flight from London to land. Because of the customs and the corruption in the country, there was no way we could do this legally. I would have done anything to try and get her well enough to get to the United Kingdom. The plan was that BEA would be given the drugs legally, and they would go through customs in London. They would then transfer them by hand to the pilots of the BOAC plane at Beruit. The BOAC agent decided that the best way was for him to go straight up to the plane when it landed as he was well known and could enter the plane, where the pilot would give him the box into his hand. If he was asked any questions, he knew what to do about paying off the customs or the police. I was standing with father and another man outside the buildings in the shadow of the few trees they had growing in what was meant to be a small garden, waiting for the agent to arrive. However, as life would have it, he was nowhere to be seen when the plane landed. There was plenty of movement around the plane as it was checked and the luggage was taken off and new luggage put on, plus the food for the next leg of its journey. A window in the cockpit opened, and a hand waved out, signalling to come. Well, I just did it; I walked very quickly across the expanse of the tarmac up to the front of the plane. Someone from above me dropped a box into my hands and said 'best of luck', and I walked back to the cover of the tree. I am sure my heart must have been so loud that it could be heard all around me. The agent arrived in time to pop me into a car, and we drove off to the hospital. He had been held up inside the building with clients who were getting on to the plane. I never doubted him, but I wished he had been there to get the medicines and not me.

I had another interesting incident. The head doctor of the hospital visited me regularly in my room to see how things were progressing. One day, he told me he had been speaking to a very good friend who had gone through medical school with him in South Africa, a Dr Bernard. I had, of course, heard about him; he had recently done the first heart transplant. He was travelling to London to give lectures and was coming to stay with the doctor when he visited Abadan. He wanted to see May. It was a very short visit, at least when I was there. But he did tell me that a cure would be found some day. He also told me that pancreas, heart, and lung transplants would be the way forward, maybe not in May's lifetime, but in the future. Of course, he was correct up to a point. Some the children who have CF now do get heart and lung transplants, which prolong their lives.

We had many ups and downs over the period of six months that May spent in the hospital in Abadan. May slowly improved. Her cough came back, and that pleased the doctors? This meant that the mucus gathering in her lungs was now not clinging to them so much. Often she was able to cough up the sticky mucus, and although it was distressing for her, being sick was another way she got rid of it. She could not walk very far, just a few steps, but anything was an improvement.

I have to admit that even though I had spent months in the hospital, I have no real recollection of what shape it was. I really only saw the small room that May was in and the ward that she seemed to be part of. I just got the impression that it was apart from the entrance building made up of long low buildings.

At the end of June, Alex told me that at last the large box, the size of a double bed and about six feet high, had arrived by barge from Abadan. It was our household goods that had been sent by ship way back in December. I also got the news from the doctors that they felt May was as good as they could get her and that she would be able to fly to London by the middle of July. A doctor would travel with us and she would be going to the Great Ormand Street Hospital in London. I was over the moon; not only were we getting to travel to the United Kingdom, but she was going to the best children's hospital in the world.

I had to get back to Mashar to pack up for the journey home, and, of course, I wanted to see my own possessions in my home in Mashar. I had no idea when that would be, but I wanted something to remember when I wasn't there. The doctors said to go for a week or two and get myself a break. I had been living in the hospital for all those months with only a night away, when Alex came through, which wasn't every week, but when his shift allowed. On one of the earlier visits he told me that the puppy had to be put to sleep, unfortunately, because he was working and it was being left alone. It had started to demolish the furniture etc. He also told me that Shona and John had to put their dog, which was from the same litter, to sleep, as it was biting.

It was nice to be back in Mashar. I had, by now, gotten used to the fact that I wasn't in Scotland or even the United Kingdom. Things that had been alien to me six months ago were just normal. The Iranian nurses were all so good to May and kind and loving. One in particular used to come in on her days off, and we would take her out into the gardens of the hospital. I knew she would be all right as long as I didn't stay away too long. Well, that is what I thought. The weather was very hot, and after the air-conditioned hospital and the fact that May and I never went outside until evening, it hit me very hard. I had not adjusted slowly to the change but had become aware of it all at once. The first thing that happened when I got to the house was the children next door wanted to know when the box was to be opened, so did I. The next day was D-Day. It was so exciting to see my bits and pieces coming out of tea chests full of straw. All my china, glasses, linen, ornaments, pots, and pans appeared like magic. I couldn't remember them going in; I had no memory of what had gone into storage and what was to be shipped. I even found my recipe books. My mum wrote every week to me and I to her and my mother-in-law. I asked my mum to send me one of her recipes on the bottom of the letter as I had to make everything from scratch. You had a lump of meat, a bag of flour, etc., and you just had to get on with it. I just needed some ideas. This she did, and I wrote them down in a book and have them to this day. That night, we slept in our own double bed for the first time since the middle of December in Scotland—what heaven! Too soon, my time was over; my bags packed for the United Kingdom, and I was on my way back to the hospital in Abadan. Whenever my tickets were ready and my visas and passport were back in my hands, Alex would come through to see me off. Once back in Abadan, I could see that May was a bit down in the dumps. The doctor told me that she had been very good and the nurses were very happy with her, but she had just wanted to know when Mummy would be back. She had not gone backwards, just not gone forward.

It wasn't really surprising when you think about it; she and I had lived for each other, just the two of us, for months. When the day came for us to leave, all the doctors and sisters and nurses, who had been so good to us, were there to say goodbye. None of them knew if they would see us again, especially May. The strange thing was, as I have said, I never thought at that time that I would lose May. If she was supposed to die, it would have been in January or February. Now it was July, and although she was still skin and bone, she was able to stand up and take a few steps and we were London-bound. Daddy kept her close in his arms all the way to the airport. He would see us at the end of September, he kept saying. I knew he was worried that he would never see her again. I kept trying to reassure him that he would, and we would be all right when we got to London. I wanted to weep, to cling to him, and never let him go, but I could not do that. I did not have the luxury of departures as seen in films and on TV. I just smiled a wan smile, kissed him hard, and let him go. No tears to be seen—they would be for my own time.

Chapter 18

London, July 1966—The World Cup

We arrived in London in July 1966, the World Cup season. I have to say that the flight was really very uneventful. The doctor sent to look after May was a bit under the weather most of the time. However, he wasn't required to look after her. In fact, at one point, on our way back from the toilet, when we got back to our seat, May wanted to know what was wrong with the doctor as he had a towel over his face.

Once we arrived in London, the pilot made an announcement, asking the passengers to remain in their seats as a very sick child was on board. They were to disembark once the child had left. May was looking for the sick child! The door of the plane was opened, and an ambulance arrived at the bottom of the steps. A nurse, a hostess, and an ambulance man came up the steps, and within a minute, one of the air hostesses arrived at the seat with the three in tow. May, the doctor, and I were ushered very gently out of the plane. I thanked the cabin crew for their help and support and went down the stairs into the ambulance. We went round to the back of the Arrivals building; the hostess took our passports and the doctor's visa and disappeared into the building. She was back in a matter of minutes. She handed us our passports and the visa said goodbye, and off we went to London. The nurse fascinated me; she had a pink-and-white striped nurse's dress on and a white starched cap, which was finished in a fantail at the back. She was really nice, and May appeared to be very comfortable with her. The speed the ambulance was travelling at made it rock from side to side and I don't know how I managed to stay on the seat, but I did. Into London we went, siren blaring, just like in the TV programmes. When we arrived, the Doctor in Admissions was very good; however, the young Iranian doctor was not much help to them as he knew no English and I knew no Farsi. May's doctor in Abadan had sent a letter, so that was some help. By the time she was admitted and the young doctor and I left in a taxi for the Bedford Hotel in Southampton Row, which is near the hospital, it was about 8.30 p.m.

When we arrived, the receptionist said there was no booking for us. I had the letter saying two single rooms were booked for that day, but, there just wasn't a room available. I was very tired, both physically and mentally. I could not get the doctor to understand, and eventually, I lost my temper and asked for the head receptionist. When he came, he was less than helpful. He explained that it was the World Cup season, and all the rooms were taken. He could get two single rooms for us in one of their other hotels, the Tavistock, in Tavistock Square, which was not far away. I told them in no uncertain terms that they would be hearing from Rank and Kuhn and the oil company in the morning. We went off in a taxi to the Tavistock, and eventually, I got into a room. I was exhausted, but I did enjoy the bath and the meal I had sent up—my first British meal since I left in December, seven months ago. It was like nectar from the gods. I was up with the lark the next morning and went down to the restaurant for my breakfast. The young Iranian doctor had not appeared, and so after I had eaten, I went to the reception to find out about him. He had gone off early in the morning, about 6 a.m., to get his flight home. I then went up to my room and phoned Rank and Khun, the travel business that dealt with the company and had supplied the letter of reservation for the doctor and myself. They were aghast that we had been treated the way we had. The oil company had a floor of rooms paid for, and even though we had arrived after the 8 p.m., it should not have made any difference. Oilmen arrived at all times of the day and night and so our rooms should have been available for us. I was not very gracious. I had telephoned them the previous night when still in the Bedford and got an answer machine, which was of no use to me. I was actually booked in for an unspecified number of days, and it was really very bad of the hotel. I was asked if I wished to go back to the Bedford. I said, 'Yes, I would' as it was handier and on the main road and not as isolated as the Tavistock. It would be easier for me to walk home in the evening. A representative from the company arrived with a car and took me back to the Bedford. When I got into the hotel, they were all apologetic about what had happened. In fact, at one point, they tried to put the blame on me. They said I had not said I was from the oil company, which was quite wrong. They had the letter in their hands and chose not to read it. I showed them that maybe to them I was a young Scottish woman but I was not going to let them off with any apology, and I told them I wasn't interested in what they said. I hoped that their family never got the treatment I did on the previous night. The young man from the company said to the manger, who had arrived, that in all probability, they would lose their contract. The excuse from the manager was probably nearer to the truth than any other. The World Cup was putting a strain on the availability of rooms in London.

Once I was settled in, I went off to Great Ormand Street. May was sitting up in her cot in a small section with four beds. She was so pleased to see me and became a bit weepy. The doctor and a nurse came to see me, and the nurse stayed with May while I went off with the doctor to discuss May's condition. They were wonderful; I cannot ever thank them enough for all they did for May. She was immediately put on to a regime of physiotherapy, called postural drainage (Tips and Taps was what they called it). She was put on a special no-fat, high-carbonate diet, and she was given a special powder to be eaten before she ate her food (the pancreas of a boar). That and the antibiotics would help to keep her as free as they could of infection in her lungs. I learnt such a lot from that time in London. The doctors spoke to me; however, none of the doctors who dealt with May ever tried to make me feel they could make her better—too much damage had been done to her lungs. The first thing they did in the morning was to give her X-rays. She had lost the use of the base of both lungs. They were badly damaged by the pneumonia she had had. They were very professional, but I knew from their reactions that they were quite taken aback that the doctor in Dundee had not seen her when she had the infection and he had presumed that she had measles. Also, they thought that DRI should have tested her for CF. It was a simple test, which would probably have told them she had it. They take a sample of sweat and test it for salt, its salt content, so I was told; if high, it indicated CF. Of course, they didn't actually say anything, but they kept questioning me about my time with Margaret and May before we left the United Kingdom. They had nothing but praise for the hospital in Abadan; they had done the best they could have done under the circumstances. None of them had ever seen or treated CF. The big change for me was her physiotherapy. I was taught how to do it and explained that it was imperative that she have it at that time every day at least five times. She lay on her tummy over a mound of pillows with her head and feet on the mattress. Then the physiotherapist, using cupped hands, quite firmly patted her sides in the vicinity of her lungs, first one side, then the other. This loosened the sticky mucus that filled her lungs and made her cough up the sticky mucus, which was very prone to infection. At first, May did not like this being done, mainly because it made her sick. However, she had to get used to it, and she did. As she began to get stronger, she was more able for the therapy. That and the powder before her meals meant that she began to put on some weight. She and I felt like pincushions as we were always getting blood taken from us. This was all for research into the condition. I had to leave her every night after her tea; there were no visiting hours that I noticed, but maybe May's condition meant that I was allowed in any time. I am not sure.

The evening of my first whole day in London, I went back to the Bedford for my evening meal. After the meal, I took my coffee into one of the lounges. I had just got seated when a middle-aged man came across and started to speak to me. I did not encourage any conversation; I just got up and walked out. I was not happy; the hotel was full of men watching the World Cup football. It was not the family hotel that Captain Rogers said I was going to when he came to see me before I left Abadan. The following night, I wandered down Southampton Row and saw a number of restaurants. I liked the look of a French one; it had an awning outside, and I could see checked tablecloths. I decided to try it. The waiter was very nice and friendly, and we got talking. He asked me if I was on holiday, and I explained why I was there. Before I left after my meal, the chef appeared. He told me to come in every night and they would keep me a table and I would not pay the full amount for the meal; they would give me a discount. I was so overwhelmed, I admit to crying. I had not realised just how lonely I was. I had never been alone anywhere until I went to Aga Jari and then on to Abadan. I had never been to London before; I had spent months in an alien environment in a foreign country. I was away from my husband, my family, and I began to realise I was alone with all the worry and responsibility on my very small shoulders. The hand of friendship overwhelmed me. I did go in every night, and I was so lucky to have found a haven where I could sit over my meal and be looked after. They all became my friends.

I decided that I was not going to stay in the Bedford. It was costing me an arm and a leg, and I worked out how much it was in the week—some £85, which was a great deal in 1966. I found a smaller hotel a little bit further away from the hospital, but still within walking distance. I moved in on Saturday, so I was less than a week at the Bedford. I received a letter then from one of Alex's friends' wives. I knew her as she had been brought up in a street very close to where I lived in Dundee and we had gone to the same schools. She was a teacher and had decided to come down to London before she went back to school. I booked her into a room in the hotel, and I was so pleased to have her company for a few days. She was able to go back to Scotland and tell both sets of parents how things were. While she was there, we decided that the hotel was still too expensive, so she did a hotel hunt round the hospital area. She found me a bit of a scruffy but clean room in a hotel called The Celtic Hotel; it was just minutes from the hospital. It was the best move, as even though it wasn't first class—in fact it wasn't even third class—but the couple who ran it were so kind. Whenever I arrived back in the evening, they would be watching to find out how things were. She arranged for my washing to be done for practically nothing, and I was very content staying with them until I left London.

May started to improve very slowly as first, but I could see her getting a little bit stronger every day. I was allowed to take her out in one of the hospital pushchairs. She had no clothes that fitted her, so she wore the hospital's clothes. I had to cover her up and keep her cosy, even though it was now into

August and coming up to her birthday. What a three years it had been! It had all started out with such joy and self-assurance that life was going to be good. I learnt never to take anything for granted, least of all life itself. There was a park quite near and I took her there, and gradually she wanted to sit on the swing. Wonderful! Then we would just walk around just like a normal mummy and child, except there was nothing normal about us. The child lived in a hospital and I in a hotel. Her birthday was low-key; she had cards from the family and toys from me, and balloons. A few weeks later, the doctors decided that she was ready to go to the convalescent home belonging to the hospital. They had done as much as they could do for her in London, and it was a case of more of the same; only time would tell us what the end was. Tadworth Court in the village of Tadworth in Surrey was our next stop.

Chapter 19

Tadworth Court

When we were getting organised to go to Surrey, I was told that I would be placed with a family who were members of the 'Friends of Tadworth Court'. They lived in the village just a walk away from the home. We were to travel down mid morning by car. The night before, I said goodbye to my friends in the restaurant and thanked them for their kindness. It was quite emotional as they were all French, and a lot of hugging and kissing went on and prayers and hopes for the future. Then I had to go through it all again at the hotel, this time it was an Irish goodbye. I always say that these people between them saved me from what could have been the loneliest time of my life.

I had my own clothes and May's in the two cases I had brought from Abadan. May's weren't much use to her, but I had added some to mine. Well, you couldn't be in London and not buy clothes, could you?

We arrived at Tadworth Court late in the afternoon, and it was a lovely place. The old house was still used for nurses and doctors and as the office. Kitchen, laundry, all seemed to be there. The wards were all purpose-built. They were built around a courtyard. When you walked in the door of May's ward, you turned left into the corridor. It had a suite of rooms for parents on the left side and on the right were cupboards and doors that I never saw in except the end door, which was the sister's office. Two sides of this room had glass windows which overlooked the ward, so she could see everything that was going on. The end of the corridor opened out into a large, bright, airy ward. Both the sides and one end of the ward were all-glass windows; the other end housed the kitchen, toilets, bathrooms, and sluices. From what I saw of the place, all the wards were the same, built round quadrangles with gardens in the middle. If this is not correct, then my memory must be playing tricks with me.

I got May settled into her new surroundings and met her new physiotherapists who gave her, her 'tips and taps'. Then we had tea. It was made in the kitchen by the nurses, and did we enjoy it—fish fingers, beans, and bread and butter with jam. Then I bathed her, and she was ready for bed. A lady arrived to take me to her home. Edna Mullet. Well, all I can say is that from the moment she shook my hand, we clicked. May was on the weepy side and standing at the bottom of her bed, sobbing her heart out. I knew she would be fine once I left as I had seen other children do this when in London. Edna was upset to see May. She was still so extremely thin with matchstick arms and legs and an extended tummy, but she was nothing like as bad as she had been when I brought her home. We left, and she drove me the short distance and showed me the way to walk the next day. I was met by her husband, Peter, and her daughters, Wanda and Lesley. I was shown my room and where the 'loo' was. They would be watching TV in the lounge and I could come down when I wanted to. 'No hurry. Just make yourself at home.' Supper wasn't for a while. The house was a detached villa, set in a large garden. Edna didn't work, but Peter was with the Ford Motor Company. I don't know if he sold the cars or was in the office. He drove a large Ford car, top of the range with a fancy name, and Edna drove a small family Ford. They had both been in the RAF during the war years. That was where they met. They were in their forties if not nearer fifties. We got into a routine; I had breakfast and laid out any washing that required doing. Edna had a lady who came in and did the washing. Then I walked to the Home, where I spent the day playing with the children and folding up clean nappies and children's clothes from the laundry. Lunch came from the kitchen, and tea we made ourselves. I ate with the children. I came home after May was bedded. I had been taught how to do May's 'tips and taps', and I did them when I was there, before her lunch and tea. Sometimes they would give me a rest and do it for me, also to check how she was progressing. As the month moved from August into September, I knew that it was going to be a long time before May was well enough to leave the home. I began to feel that I could not stay for months with Edna and Peter. It wasn't fair on them. Also, Alex was due home in October for seven or eight weeks. I spoke to the sister about it. Also, I was doing nothing but spending money, and that was a worry. Sister got me a job in the laundry if I wanted it. She would have liked me to have been made a ward helper, but I wasn't allowed to do that because May was in the Home. I spoke to Edna and Peter about this. They were very happy for me to stay with them, but if I wanted to try my hand in the laundry to see how I got on, they said, 'Well, have a go.' I was going to stay in the Home in the parents' room attached to the ward. I could make my own breakfast and would eat in the canteen at lunchtime, then eat with May in the ward at teatime. They all thought this a good idea as May was very dependent on me. So I moved out of Edna's with the promise that I would come with them anywhere they were going on a Saturday and Sunday. The laundry work was physical, and I struggled to do it. I had never done anything like it in my life. May was now able to get out with me to Edna's house for afternoon tea on a Sunday. I walked her over if it was a nice afternoon, or Peter or Edna came for us if it was bad. On one of these afternoons, Peter said I was to give up the work and they wanted me to move back in with them. Especially as Alex was coming home, he wasn't going to have us moving into some hotel when we had become part of the family. Everyone was adamant and he had already spoken to the sister. It was all arranged. I was not aware of myself. My whole life for nearly ten months had been hospitals and May. I now realised that I was as thin as May and only weighed some 7st 8lb. Sister made me go on the scales to prove the point. I was really glad to stop working; it just wasn't for me. I was told to look for a Christmas job in some of the shops in one of the surrounding towns after Alex went back. But my home was with the Mullets. All I had to do now was look forward to Alex coming home.

Chapter 20

A Leave to Remember, October 1966

May and I were really excited about Daddy coming; I hoped that he would see a big difference in his wee daughter. Every day she seemed to get a bit stronger, but it was hard for me to see a big change as I saw her all the time. I knew that the doctor—the specialist in CF and May's doctor—wanted to have a long talk about how she was getting on and the future. Sister had asked me if we had ever discussed what we thought the future would bring. I honestly told her no. I explained that we were still trying to get over the death of Margaret when I began to see the signs in May. Unfortunately, apart from the odd visits to Abadan over the next six months, we really did not have time to think about the future. We were living just a day at a time, and all my thoughts were to get her home to the United Kingdom. I knew I really did not want to bring another child into the world that had CF. I had watched both my girls suffer so much that even before May's illness I had more or less made up my mind. I wanted to be sterilised, but I knew that Alex had to give his approval and sign the consent form, and I had no idea when we could ever get round to even thinking about that. We would just have to put our faith in God and be as careful as we could when he was home. It was one of the odd things about a life like ours—Alex being at sea for the first three years of our marriage and then another year away in Abadan before we started to live together as a family. Then we were separated again almost immediately. We had really only lived together for probably less than two years as man and wife in our five years of marriage. Our love for each other was still as strong as ever, and the sexual attraction had not diminished. In 1966, the pill was in its infancy and abortion was legal in certain cases. However, I didn't have the time or the inclination to worry about the future; I was still trying to live each day as it came with all the ups and downs of CF. Some days, May was great, just a normal little girl, then the next day she would be coughing and be sick. She would have a temperature and would be unable to get anything up from her little lungs. I knew that her being sick was not a bad thing as it helped to clear her inside of the sticky mucus from her pancreas. However, some days one felt that we were taking one step forward and two steps back. Yet she was so much better than when we arrived in London.

We were counting the days, then the hours, to Daddy coming home. I left in the morning by train to travel up to London and then went to Heathrow. I was in plenty of time for the plane and was at the Arrivals lounge, waiting for him to come through. He looked great, tanned and golden in colour, and seemed large to me. He was over six feet but carried no superfluous fat. I just clung on to him but tried to be as happy as I could be as I did not want to spoil his coming home. We got the train back to London. We took time out to go for a meal together, just to give him all the news etc. Then we went down to Surrey. It was, by this time, seven in the evening and too late to go to the Home, so we went to Edna and Peter's. They were waiting for us with open arms. We had a long leisurely meal that night with all his news about the job and the people. Peter was interested in our life. The social life seemed to be the hub of our existence—the lunches, suppers, dinners, bridge parties (not that Alex went to these), and, of course, the golf and the Golf Club. He made it sound better than it was to me, but, of course, I hadn't really had time to get into anything before I had to leave. Even before May took ill, my time was all on her and trying to get back to being as normal as possible after Margaret.

The next morning, we walked to the Home. Alex was very quiet; I think he was afraid of what he was going to see. I realised by then that he did take quite a lot of drink to shut out the past and the future. He did not know what was going on at home, and that was the terrible thing. However, he was home now and we were together, and I was going to do everything in my power to keep us so. He was surprised with the Home and the ward. Of course, May couldn't remember him right away, but once she had been cuddled and kissed, she was telling everyone who would listen, that her daddy was here. Once again life took on a steadier look. We visited from after breakfast to begin with until after tea. Then we started to go to London sometimes in the morning and arrive back in the middle of the afternoon. Sometimes we took May out for a walk in the gardens and visited the pigs and their babies, which she was desperate to show to Daddy as she and I went there most days. Also the hens, and sometimes, we went further afield, and she saw sheep and cows in the fields. Our walks got longer as his stay progressed. One day, we took her to Chessington Zoo. That was a dream come true for us—to be out as a family, something I never thought would happen ever again. It was a beautiful autumn day. The sun was shining, and the countryside was beautiful. We had a wonderful time; May was so happy. She laughed at the animals and so enjoyed herself that we could not be anything but happy with her. Alex was taught how to do the postural drainage (tips and taps) but was afraid he would hurt May. He knew that if I was unable to do them for any reason he had to be able to do them. Her life depended to a very large part on the therapy. We sometimes did the therapy before tea and always before bed.

Sister informed us about two weeks into Alex's leave that May's doctor wanted to have a talk with us. I did not know what he was going to tell us or say to us. There were one or two very serious things that came out of that consultation. Firstly, May's condition. He was not sure if or how she would survive out of a hospital environment. The prognosis was not good. Her lungs were very severely damaged, and they were having great difficulty in removing the mucus. There was no chance of clearing her lungs completely. That meant that she would be very prone to any infection she came up against. They wanted to give her a measles vaccination; she had never had measles—so much for the doctor in Dundee. What she had had was pneumonia, and that and the two more bouts in Mashar, along with the malfunctioning of the pancreas, had done irreparable damage to the lungs. It would take a long time to get her fit enough to be transferred to Scotland, but as soon as they were satisfied, they would try and get us back up home to our family. He asked me how many pregnancies I had since my marriage. I said three and I did conceive very easily.

'We want you to have another child,' he said. 'We would monitor you all the way through and be there for you all the time.'

I was adamant that I did not want to bring into the world another child with CF. He asked Alex about his brother's family.

'Three girls,' said Alex.

'*Mmmm!*' said the doctor. We were told that sometimes a change in the sex of a baby meant they were born free of CF. However, as the sex was the male sperm and because Alex's brother had three daughters, our chance of a change was doubtful.

He asked if we were interested in artificial Insemination from a donor.

'No,' said Alex. 'Definitely *no*.' Alex asked about adoption and told him we had discussed it long before we had any family and that was the route we wanted to go down. He said that he would do what he could for us. He did not want us to make May our life as we had no way of knowing how long that would be. He said that he was one of the doctors for an adoption society in London and he would speak to them. He was very nice, and although it was awful to have to face the truth, he did somehow make us feel that we did have a future and he would be there for us whatever it held.

Within days, the sister came to say that the doctor had been on the phone and we were to go to an address in Croydon for a meeting with the Council

Adoption Department there for an interview with a view to being put on the adoption list. It was a terrible day with rain pelting down. When we arrived, we went to a cafe for a cup of coffee as we were a bit early. When we left the cafe, the rain had stopped, and as we stood there deciding which way to go, a woman passed us, pushing what looked like a teenage girl on what looked like a hospital trolley. We both looked at each other, and Alex took hold of my hand and squashed it gently. He looked me in the eye and said, 'We are so lucky. We can go all the way to the zoo for a day out and no one is any the wiser that she has anything wrong with her. We are lucky.' Then he gave me a hug, and off we went to the interview. It was the most unsatisfactory interview I have ever had. The woman's telephone never stopped ringing. One of the conversations stuck with me; it was as if she was selling a lump of meat. I am sure she was arranging to have a baby placed in a family. We did not see anything about this woman that made us feel that what she was doing was so important to the baby, never mind the couple who want to adopt. We left there quite depressed, knowing we wanted nothing to do with Croydon Social Services.

We were soon lifted from our depression and back up again as the doctor sent a letter to us, telling us that an interview had been arranged at a London adoption society. Alex and I went up to London for the first Interview. It was nerve-wracking to say the least. We arrived at what I think must have been a town house in the 1800s but was now an office. We were shown into a waiting room, but within minutes, a lady came in and introduced herself as Mrs Cunningham, the secretary, and offered us a tea or a coffee. It was all very different from our trip to Croydon. We refused but thanked her, and she sat down and we had a conversation with her. She spoke of her family and asked all about May and our family in Scotland. Then we were shown into a boardroom, which was full of ladies and gentlemen, all sitting round this vast table. Once the introduction was done, one of the ladies started to ask us about our own backgrounds. How Alex was in Iran. All our principles were queried. Our ideas were put to the test. Our opinions asked. When we left that room, my lasting impression was of a large table with rounded corners, shiny and brown. All these people sitting around, all at an age of our parents with what we expected would be their mindset. I was terrified that I had said the wrong thing, but Alex seemed to be quiet and calm. Maybe, like me, he was in turmoil inside. We were not told anything that afternoon, but within a week, we had a letter to say that we had passed the first interview. May knew that we were looking for a baby brother or sister for her. The sister on the ward was over the moon when we got the letter as she was so aware of May's condition.

Alex had only three weeks left of his leave; it was decided that we should go up to Scotland to my family and his for two weeks. I had not been away from a hospital since January, and although the doctor had tried to get me to go up home to Dundee for a weekend not long after I arrived in London, I would not go. One of his young doctors, Dr Brown, came from Dundee and had been at the Harris Academy with me, and the doctor knew that he was going up to Dundee for a long weekend. He said he would arrange for him to take and bring me back. I just would not leave May at that time. By October, I felt she was still very fragile but was able to be left on her own with all the care and attention she would get at the Home and with Edna and Peter on hand. So all was put in place for our trip home. We were going to stay with my mum and dad. We did tell May we were off for a few days, and we asked her, if she was a good girl, what she would really like. 'A baby' was her reply, and so I said we would bring her a baby doll and she could dress and undress it all the time. She was quite happy with that, and we got away without any bother. Cases packed, and off we went.

Chapter 21

Scotland and More Trouble

We took the train from King's Cross to Dundee; my dad was waiting for us there. We decided to hire a car for the two weeks so we could be independent, and it was one of the first things we did the next day. We were to stay with my mum and dad for one week then go down to Alex's for the second. On our first visit to his mum and dad, I felt that something was wrong. Alex's mum was preoccupied with something. But Dad was his usual self when he came in from work. However, she wasn't as interested in how May was or in anything to do with our life. I heard a lot about Andy and what he was doing. I couldn't put my finger on what was wrong, but as Alex seemed happy enough, I said nothing. One day when Andy came in to their mum's and we were alone, he told me that Dad was having an affair. Dad was denying it, said that she was a customer, and he was making loose covers for her. Andy said that Dad had been seen by someone coming out of the flats in Lochee and also in a bar in Lochee with a woman. There were one or two things that were plausible. She could genuinely be a customer, as he had to visit the homes of customers to measure and fit the loose covers. However, being seen in a bar was the last thing I would have thought as normal for Dad. On the way home, I told Alex what Andy had said. He was very angry at Andy. He said that Andy had no right to say what he said and that Dad was not having an affair with anyone. Alex said that Andy should have had more sense than to pass on gossip to me. I had enough on my plate without getting my head filled with anything else. We were trying to come to terms with the fact that May's life was to be short. Did his brother not realise that we were living with a time bomb and that May's prognosis was the worst it could be? I have very rarely seen Alex annoyed or angry, but that night he was. After that he spoke to my mum and dad, and it was decided we would not stay at his mum's. The thing that always amazed me was she wasn't even bothered. Apart from that, we had a very nice time with my parents. We were nearly at the end of our stay. We had finished all Alex's shopping and he was ready for another Year. All too soon for my mum and dad, we were on our way back down. It had been a very different kind of break from the one I had hoped for.

It was now mid-November and a year since Margaret's death. We had a lovely welcome back from Edna, Peter, and the girls. May was so pleased to see us, and, as before, she did not go backwards, but she didn't progress either when we were away from her. We bought her two baby dolls, and she immediately undressed them and put them to bed. That told us a lot about what she thought life was all about. I made up my mind that I would be with her and would not leave her for more than a day again.

I had hoped that we would have our next interview with the adoption society in London before Alex left for Iran, but it didn't materialise. We went to Sutton one day as I had applied for a job over the Christmas time in Boots, and I got the job. I was to start in the first week in December. I always kept my feelings to myself, and on the whole on his previous departures I had been very good as I always had something to look forward to. However, this time, I really didn't want Alex to leave, but I knew I couldn't let him know that. I knew he was thinking about May and whether would he ever see her again. Also, He would be alone at Christmas. The other thing was his mum.

All the time I had been in Iran, I had written a letter every week to both my mum and his mum. My mum, in return, wrote every week and also sent Alex *The Sunday Post*, which arrived two or three weeks later. Alex's mum did not write every week, but she did so at regular intervals. Since my arrival in London, I had phoned both mums on a Sunday night. Then when I was settled down with Edna, both mums had been the ones to phone as I was always at Edna's on Sunday at teatime. My mum did so every week without fail; however, Alex's mum often waited nearly a month before phoning me, and so I often had to do the phoning. When we came back to Tadworth, Alex had only a week left. Alex decided to phone his mum about two days before he left, but he got no reply. He tried on and off all that evening but never got any reply. The next day, he tried calling her, but always there was no reply. He even phoned telephone enquiries to see if there was something wrong with the phone, but it was OK. All the last day I could see him getting more and more agitated as there was still no reply. His brother did not have a phone at that time. He even tried at the airport. I was by this time so annoyed with her. Surely, if she was going away to Glasgow for a few days to visit family, she would have said something when we last spoke to her before coming south? Surely she wouldn't let her son go way for a whole year, knowing as she must, that he was leaving his very ill little girl behind? Well, he never did get through to her, and once again she completely astounded me by her behaviour.

Saying goodbye to Alex was so very difficult; I did not want him to know that my heart was breaking. How could I when I knew his was breaking too! His mum had been the final blow in a leave that had far more downs than ups. I was so annoyed at his mum that I decided not to even try to contact her. I waited for his mum to phone for nearly three weeks; then Edna said one Sunday night that I must try and get through to her. I did, and she answered. There was no talk about Alex being away, nothing about not phoning. She just answered right in with 'Dad is having an affair. He says he isn't, but I know he is'. The rest of the call was all about her life with him etc., etc. Yet she said she wanted him back. I came off the phone shattered. When I told Edna and Peter what I had had listened to, Edna's reaction was 'What a selfish woman'. I never phoned her again but wrote every two weeks, and if I got replies, they were few and far between. So I can't remember or even guess what she wrote. I think I decided then that I really had enough on my plate without her.

I started my job and did enjoy the routine. I bought and took into the ward for the little girls there little sachets of bubble bath, and they all got one in their baths at night. What excitement, I can tell you. You have to remember that some of them had been there for months, so anything that was different was wonderful for them. I would try and bring in something different for them. One night I was late in finishing and with very little time to catch my bus, I had no time to buy them anything. Well, would you believe it, May had a right tantrum. You could have knocked me down with a feather. I was quite shocked, but underneath I was so pleased; it showed her fighting spirit.

May on Trampoline, Meadow Ward,
Tadworth Court, Surray 1966
(Great Ormand Street, Convalescent Home)

On the Trampoline with another
C.F. little boy

Chapter 22

Christmas 1966

Christmas 1966 was like no other Christmas I ever had up to then or since. Over the Christmas period, all the children who were well enough were allowed to go home. May wasn't getting home, but I knew we would not. There was a baby that I can remember and I think two or maybe three other children. I had been asked if I would like to stay in the Home for the night so I could be with May in the morning. I don't know if the other parents were offered accommodation or not. I jumped at the chance. I brought all the gifts that had been sent from home and the ones Alex and I had bought her and those from the Mullets and my clothes for the day. It may seem a strange thing to say, but I had one of the happiest and most meaningful Christmas Eve and Christmas Day ever. The ward was all decorated and had a real Christmas tree. The nurses had the place looking really lovely. On Christmas Eve, we hung the stockings at the end of the cots. Then we could hear singing coming from other parts of the Home. A group of off-duty nurses and sisters plus the odd doctor came into the ward singing carols. The lights were low, and somehow the atmosphere was just right for 'Away in a Manger' and 'Silent Night'. I was very moved by the whole thing. Somehow it seemed far more important to me than in previous years. Before going to bed, I brought the big Santa sack I had bought into the ward and put it into the kitchen. On Christmas morning, I was up with the lark and peeped in to the ward, still in my night attire. The night staff was just beginning to prepare breakfast, so I went in to help them until May woke. I had put her presents at the foot of her bed and helped the nurses put the other children's out. I had made up a box for the nurses and got perfume for the sister.

There was great excitement when May woke to her presents, just like any other three-year-old. One of the routines of the ward was all the children old enough to dress themselves did so. All the clothes were laid out at the end of the cot, and they got on with it. I never changed that routine from that time onward. May got dressed while I helped serve breakfast, and we all had a jolly time that morning. I went off to get myself dressed before the day shift came on. I had just got into my room when the sister appeared. After a Christmas greeting, she produced a nurse's uniform—striped dress and white apron and the fantail hat, which I was told I had to wear for the day! What fun we had, me trying to impress May and the doctors, but I didn't fool any of them. During the morning, I was told that the matron would be coming down from London to visit all the children still in the Home. Of course, being Christmas, there wasn't a large staff on the ward, only three plus me. Later that morning, there was a lot of noise like something being wheeled along the corridor, and in came matron, pushed on a trolley by two doctors and escorted by some of the nurses.

After she had spoken to the little ones and had seen their presents she looked up and said, 'I believe we have a new nurse on today. I had better inspect her to make sure she comes up to scratch.' So that is how I met the lady who helped to make Great Ormand Street Hospital such a wonderful place. She was really kind and said that she had been told about me by the doctor. She hoped that I was not missing my husband and family too much, but from what she had heard, she was sure that I would be making the very best of the day. I was quite speechless, but I did say something in the way of a thank you for her kind words. Then she got back on her trolley and left to the singing of 'We wish you a Merry Christmas'. We had a lovely lunch; I had to go to the big house for it with the one of the nurses. Obviously, it was done in two shifts. There was a lot of banter from the doctors and nurses when I went in. It was just all fun and plenty of laughter. It reminded me of the fun times I had with my fellow Guiders in what seemed ages ago. Then I came back to the ward to make sandwiches and set out the fancy cakes. It was an open day at the Home, and the other children were visited by parents and families in the afternoon. I was to help with the teas etc. Well, I was told that 'you can't be dressed as an nurse and sit on your bottom'. Edna and Peter came with the girls to join in the fun, and May was so pleased to see them. One of the nurses and myself were making more tea in the kitchen when one of the visitors came in and said, 'Nurse, is there anymore tea?' I calmly took the teapot and filled up her cup. What giggles we had! I really didn't look anything other than someone in a nurse's uniform. Not long after that, a great buzz set up; a rumour rang around that someone special was coming very soon. There was a lot of 'who' 'who' mostly from the relations and friends. Then a bell was heard ringing, and of course, in walked Santa Claus. This was the icing on the cake of a wonderful day for at least one little girl and her mum. May's gift was a horse. It had a head and its body was a pole with handle bars at the neck and two wheels at the end. It had a lovely head and eyes, and she learnt very quickly to put it between her legs and run about and pretend she was riding it. It moved very easily over the floor on its wheels, so she wasn't even tired. I was told it was a hobby horse. I got a necklace and a kiss from Santa. Once everyone was away and we had settled down, I changed into my own clothes. Not long after that we had more visitors to the ward. May's doctor came in with his wife and boys. May was sitting up in bed, and I was reading her a book when he walked in. I noticed immediately that one of the boys had Down's syndrome. I realised that he did know what he was saying when he told Alex and me not to make May our life but to have more children. Somehow it made me feel as if he really did understand what the parents of the children whose lives he was trying to save, or at least give them a better life for as long as they lived, were going through. They were such a happy family that Christmas evening, so full of laughter and joy that transmitted itself to all of us. Somehow it was a fitting end to a wonderful day.

After the excitement of Christmas and New Year, life once again had some sense of normality to it, or maybe I should say it was as normal as it had been for a year. For the New Year, I was invited to join Edna and Peter at a neighbour's house for a party. I put on my 'little black dress' and went off with them. It was quite something for me as I had not been out socially for many, many months. I enjoyed myself very much. However, at one point the lady of the house came to make herself known to me.

'Are you the mother living with Edna?'

'Yes,' I replied.

'My, you wouldn't think anything was wrong in your life!' When I told Edna when we got home, she said that it told you something about the person. If it had been her then everyone in the room would have been told. What a happy night everyone would have had! Back to life as usual, I spent all day with May and the evenings with Edna and Peter. On Sundays, I took May for her tea to Mullets. She thought it wonderful, and so did I. She was, unfortunately, very well behaved. I say 'unfortunately' because I did realise that it was due to her condition that she sat and played so quietly, rather than run about like a normal three-year-old. However, the girls loved playing with her, and she enjoyed herself immensely. The girls were in a swimming club, and on another outing, I went and watched them swimming in competitions in their club.

Chapter 23

Good News, 1967

Two things happened at the end of January, both very exciting. The first was that I got word to go for a second interview in London at the adoption society. The second was that the doctors began to tell me that if May continued to improve, they would consider her going out to Iran to have a holiday with her daddy. It would be nice for him so see her so much better and not to remember her as she had been when he was on leave. I was over the moon on both counts.

The first problem to be faced was my trip to London. The night before my visit, just as the sister was leaving, she came to wish me good luck and said she was sure all would be well. The mother of one of the patients was listening. I had never spoken to her as she was extremely well dressed, her make-up was immaculate, and her boy was in a room on his own. She did not mix with the other mums and dads. She came over to me and said someone had told her that I wanted to adopt. She spoke down to me not as someone she thought was her equal.

'I tried to adopt, and I didn't get a child,' she informed me in no uncertain terms. 'How do you think you will get a baby? I had everything, a big house, washing machine, dishwasher, car, and plenty of money. My husband owns his own shop in London.'

I didn't answer her; I was so taken aback at her rudeness. I was leaving anyway to go back to Edna's, so I just left. However, I saw that the sister was still in her office and I knocked and she told me to come in. I told her what had happened. She told me to sit down and forget what the woman had said to me. She asked me not to repeat to anyone in the hospital what she was about to tell me, as it was confidential.

'The couple did not get a child because they wanted one as they had everything but a child. A child is not a commodity, but a human being with all the faults that everyone has. Do you know what the boy is in hospital for?'

I told her I did not know.

'Well,' she said, 'he is in because he wets the bed. There is nothing wrong with him physically to cause him to do this. We are trying to find out what is behind the wee boy's trouble, but the doctors are 100 per cent sure it all stems from his home life. You see, sometimes you only have to speak to parents to realise that the last thing they should have is children. The society she went to saw through her, and they had the doctor's report and a home visit report and refused to give her a baby on what they were told. Please don't worry. Nothing like that will happen to you. You are a loving mummy to May, and you will make a wonderful mummy to any baby they offer you.'

I went to London, feeling somehow very nervous, not knowing what was in front of me. Sitting on the train, I wondered what they would ask me; I didn't have Alex there saying all the right things. The room I was shown into was the same waiting room; however, I wasn't in it long before Mrs Cunningham, the secretary came in. I was beginning to feel I knew her as we had met the last time and she had been corresponding with me. She was in her late fifties and was so welcoming. She took me into her office and we had a cup of tea and she asked me how May was and how Alex was getting on. I was able to tell her that we hoped to go out for Easter to Bander Mashar, to see Alex. Another young woman came in to tell us the committee was waiting for us. In I went, feeling like a lamb going to the slaughterhouse. I was introduced and then left to myself. The committee appeared to me to be made up of the same elderly persons. However, I suppose that at thirty, most people looked older to me. Most of the questions were about where we would live, and I told them that once May was able to go to Scotland, I would be buying a home for us there. I said that I hoped we would all be able to go to Iran for some time during the year to be with my husband. They asked about our finances and about my family and if they were in agreement with our adopting. Did I have any interests? I told them about my Guiding. I was asked about my religious beliefs. I said that I was Church of Scotland; I had been a teacher at Sunday school, and Alex had been brought up as a Plymouth Brethren but had been baptised in the Church of Scotland. Then one of the ladies asked me, out of the blue it seemed, if I believed in smacking a child? How did I answer this? Did I say yes or did I say no? I said, 'I do not think that smacking a child was the way to reprimand them. However, if I said to them, "if you do that again I will smack you" and they persisted, then I might. Otherwise, what would be the point of saying it? However, I am sure I would use another method as I had only once been smacked myself as my parents did not believe in lifting your hand to a child. I have never smacked May. I know that Alex would never do it.' I then prayed I had said the right thing. Once the interview was over and I had shaken hands with everyone in the room and been wished all the best for the future, I left wondering if that was a good sign or a bad sign. I did not know at the time but learnt later that this doctor was the paediatric consultant for the society. I also found out at the same time that in the room there was a lady whose son was the vicar of the church in Ahvāz in south Iran, who visited Bander Mashar, Kharg Island, and Aga Jari, and I had met him at the air strip on my way to Abadan the year before! I have always believed that things that happen to you are all done for a reason. We were meant to go to that society.

The second was our impending trip to Iran. I was quite worried about how I was going to manage May in Mashar. I knew I had been well taught; I knew all about her illness, how to do the postural drainage at least four times per day and to increase it if I thought she required it. I had been doing it myself since Christmas, and she was used to me. I had all the information on her different antibiotics, and she was on a reduced amount by the time we left. I knew all about her diet; I had regular visits from the dietician, and I had been helping to make the teas at the ward since arriving in Tadworth. I also knew how many pills to give her before meals. They were enormous, and I don't know how she managed. She also got supplements of vitamins and, if my memory is correct, calcium and iron. The hospital made up a large box of all the drugs required for our two-month stay and a letter for the head doctor in Abadan, telling him all that was required if she should take ill and, if this should happen, to give me as much support as they could as I was capable of looking after her and dealing with any therapy required. I was even taught how to give an injection but hoped that I would never have to do it. I went to London and got May's clothes that I was sure she would require, although it would not be very hot as it was in March and April that we were going to be there. We both needed underwear, and I remember telling Edna of the wee shop we all went to with my mother-in-law to buy the same things before our world collapsed around us. It seemed so long ago as so much had happened in the intervening twenty months. All I did this time was visit M & S and get everything I required. We said our goodbyes to the sister and the nurses; I could not speak properly when I got May to hand a big box of chocolates and flowers and a box of chocolate biscuits for the cuppies. We had lots of cuppies and I usually made them. I was going to miss all of them very much and the security they gave me; however, we were coming straight back to Tadworth on our return.

Chapter 24

Bander Mashar, Spring 1967

Edna and Peter took us to Heathrow, and we set off on our journey; first we went to Beruit by BEA. Then we changed to a BOAC flight for Abadan. May loved the whole experience, and so did I. We had fun with the trays of food and the drinks in little bottles and, of course, the sweets when we were taking off and landing. Alex had managed, through the BOAC representative, to be waiting for us when we landed in Abadan. I did not have the panic attack going through customs that I had the first time. I was worried about the medicines, but I had mixed them in with our clothes in the cases and they really just let us through without looking at the luggage. I had, by this time, been living amongst the Iranian people—surrounded by Iranian doctors, nurses, and orderlies in the hospital—and had become used to the smells of the bazaar and the dusty grime. The taxi was waiting, and we were whisked off to the hotel and had a wash before we took May for a meal in the dining room. Chicken kebab was her desire and chicken she got followed by ice cream. That was her meal every time we went to the hotel. Why, I don't know but when asked, she said she liked it. I was so used to doing her tips and taps that it happened without any fuss. Alex was quite upset when I did it the first time before the meal, but he got used to it after a while. I could never manage to get him to do them except for the time in the future when I had to go into hospital. Next day, we went to the hospital with the letter for her doctor and met the nurses and doctors who had looked after her before. They could not believe the change in her. She looked slim but not in any way the same fragile little girl they had said goodbye to. One of them told me they thought they had sent her home to die. We made an appointment with the paediatrician for the end of March and were given a number to call if we required any help at all. A bed would be there for her and me at any time. Then we were off over the desert. May was all excited about her holiday and was busy with Daddy all the way. She had books to show him and a present for him in the case, and she also slept for quite a bit of the journey, cuddled up in his arms.

We had a lovely two months in Mashar. Alex had bought her a little bike, and she loved it and rode it everywhere we went. Of course, everyone was pleased to see us, and we got invited out a lot. As a family, we were so happy.

A few mornings after I arrived, when I was lying in my bath, I saw two feelers sticking out of the overflow between the taps, and a large cockroach dropped into the bath. When I say 'large' I mean 'large', about the size of a mouse! I never got out of a bath so quickly in my life. Then when I began to think about it, I remembered I had noticed some in the toy box and got the boy to catch them. I then went into cleansing mode, and I had all the toys and the box washed. Caliph just laughed at me, but I was afraid that they could carry a germ and pass them on to May. I even found them in the kitchen drawer. Alex said that all of the houses had them, but on talking to my neighbours, I realised they did not have as many as I did. The men decided to find out where they were nesting apart from the drains. When they went to the outside cupboard where the gardener kept his tools, they found a tea chest. Alex had given Caliph one after the sea freight had come the previous June. Instead of removing it to his home, he had kept it, straw and all, in the cupboard. It was a heaving mass of cockroaches. When they touched it, they were crawling out of it in their hundreds, and I am not exaggerating. They got it out to the street and turned it on its side. Then when the cockroaches were moving in all directions two of the men drove their cars over them. Back and forth they went until they killed as many as they could. Then the environmental men came and sprayed the whole house in one day and swept up the next. We went to sleep in one of the bachelors' houses that night while Alex went to work. It was talked about for years as one of the experiences of living in Mashar. It was the end of Caliph as Alex had had enough of him. We were sure he was taking items from the house; although it was difficult to remember everything I had in the house, I did notice things were missing. Alex made enquiries about getting another boy. We heard from one of the captains that one of the American families in Abadan was leaving, and they had a good houseboy. So we asked them to ask Jabber if he would come and see us. He came. His English was good, and he cooked and cleaned and did the ironing. He would live in and get got four days off a month, Sunday through to Thursday morning. May took to him; he told me he had four girls, no boys. Alex explained how sick May was, but that he was not to get upset if he heard her crying and coughing as might happen when she was having her therapy. What a difference! Everything was spotless, and he was able to cook meat dishes for us that weren't just 'mince and tattles'.

This time, I had more time to take stock of my surroundings. Mashar was a bit like a village, although it resembled nothing like one in the United Kingdom.

In fact, I couldn't tell you really what it looked like apart from the part I lived in. There were, if my memory is correct, around twenty-seven expatriates, with all but six, tug staff. I had more time on this holiday to look around at the people who lived and worked in Mashar. There were the superintendent in overall charge, Captain Blair, and his wife. They, I think, came from New Zealand originally. They kept to themselves, and I very rarely saw them in the time I was out. There were senior captain, Don, and his wife, Bobby. She was a good-looking woman, and you could find them on his days off at lunchtime in Vardens. Vardens was the only shop that I can remember in Mashar apart from the Staff Store. It sold anything and everything from a needle to an anchor, and if they did not have it, they could get it for you. What really drew some of the expatriates to it was the beer. You could find them at lunchtime propping up the counter and having their drink as if they were in an English pub. I liked it because he sold lovely boiled ham, which reminded me of home, and May and I loved it.

Fred and Nell Richards and two of their family lived next door to Don and Bobby, Fred being Don's engineer. Their other neighbours were Johnny Bruce and his wife; he was also an experienced captain. On the street facing the golf course, if that is what you could call it, but more about it in a minute, lived Johnny's engineer and his wife, Ruth and Pat Shaw. They were Northern Irish, and they had a very welcoming home. It was a laugh a minute when you were with them. Pat had a handbell at the side of his bed, which he would ring. Of course, there was a lot of fun as she used to say that when he rang the bell, she knew what he wanted. As they were quite old, in our eyes quite old at least, in their late forties or early fifties, we thought this funny. Poor Pat probably wanted the houseboy to take him a cup of tea, but, of course, we will never know. Next to them lived the Warrenders. Mr Warrender was a captain and they were an unusual couple as she was an Irish Catholic and he was an Irish Protestant. Next door to them was another Irish couple—Don Chalmers was an engineer, and as it was Easter holidays, his wife was out. Don was the life and soul of the party when he was on his own, but you never saw him when his wife came out. His wife was very anti-Catholic, which also meant she never went

May on Easter Picnic,
Bander Mashar
March 1967

inside her neighbour's door. Likewise, Don too never visited the neighbour, until she went away. One time when I was at home and she was either in Mashar or Abadan, she said to Alex to tell me, as she was sure I would be thrilled, that she had shaken the hand of Rev. Ian Paisley. I am sure Alex was very diplomatic, as he knew I couldn't stand the man. There was a house with contractors living in it just before you turned into our road. The Keans and their three girls lived across the road from the Mcintoshes and us. The wife was Welsh; he, I think, was English and, like Alex, an engineer and loved fun. Somewhere in another street was Bob Ray, who was a friend of Alex's, and we saw a lot of him when in Mashar. He was divorced and was friendly with the teacher. There was another captain, whose name I can't remember, and his wife, whom I met when she was a nurse in Abadan. They had two children and lived near Bob. She was also Welsh, and they were a quiet couple who also kept themselves to themselves. The last couple that I can remember were the couple from Arbroath—Mary and Philip and their small son. He was, as I have already said, a representative of the shipping agents, and after I was back home, I went to visit her mum and dad in Arbroath. They were so pleased to see May and me. I got on very well with her and used to go and visit her in the mornings. If there were others, I can't remember them after all this time, and they were probably weathermen and contractors who lived in a compound of their own. They were same who gave us the milk and the lift in the plane, which I so appreciated, and are mentioned in the next paragraph.

May on Easter Picnic,
Bander Mashar March 1967

May playing on bike in garden April 1667

May playing on bike in garden
April 1667

May playing on bike in garden
April 1667

Easter saw us on a picnic, rolling our eggs and playing games. You would not have thought May had anything wrong with her. She did get breathless if she ran about too much, but she knew her own limitations.

At the end of March, some of the American contractors who were working and living near Mashar asked Alex if we would like to be flown to Abadan for May's appointment. They had a small four-seated plane that they used to bring in fresh milk etc. The first thing these men did when I arrived was arrive at my door with two bottles of milk and a loaf of bread for May, and I got these every day while we were there. Alex said yes; it was kind of them and we would be pleased as it meant we could do it in a day. Alex was the captain of the Golf Club, and he used to say to me they want to be members and he was useful to them. However, we didn't care if they did had an alternative reason for helping; we were very grateful for everything, especially the flight. At least I was; unfortunately, Alex did not like flying. The journey was purgatory for him. We were flying only about 400 feet above the ground across a flat desert, and he was a nervous wreck. May and I enjoyed being able to see what was on the ground. Alex used to say if he was meant to fly, God would have given him wings.

When I talk about the golf course, please do not be fooled into thinking it was luscious green fairways and mirror-like greens. It was purely mudflats as fairways, and the 'greens' were a mixture of oil and sand. You could call it 'browns and darker browns'. It had nine holes, and you just went round twice. Competitions were played every Friday morning. And then a curry lunch was served. Then some of the keen members would go out again in the afternoon. All the rules about dress etc. that you found in the United Kingdom applied here and in Abadan and Kharg Island golf clubs.

The doctor was very pleased with her; she had put on weight and was a lovely colour. It was warm enough to go without a cardigan but not get sunburnt. We had to go in and see him before we left for the United Kingdom; he gave me a report to take back, but he saw no reason why she should not continue to progress.

Just about that time a letter arrived from the adoption society in London to say we had been accepted as suitable adoptive parents, and as soon as we were settled in Scotland, we were to contact them. That was a reason to have a party, so we had one in the Golf Club with the expatriates who could manage. It was not a big affair, just drinks and nibbles, and Fred Richards, as usual, did it all for me as was his kind way.

I had thought that as I was on my own with her, I would panic at the least little thing and be very fussy and worried about her. I can honestly say that I was very calm about her and did not feel the responsibility too much. I think the knowledge that I was returning to Tadworth Court helped me a great deal. Alex did worry quite a bit, but he could see for himself that she was improving and was so very happy. She took it for granted that she had to get her therapy and all her medicines; I think she thought all children were like her.

All too soon our holiday was over. They had a party for me at the Golf Club, and I was sorry to leave. Hopefully, the experiment of bringing May out was a success, and I would get out again sometime.

I had begun to think of the future. Alex and I had discussed the adoption; we wanted a boy if possible, and if I was allowed to go back to Scotland with May, then I was to go ahead and buy a home and see if we could have a baby before he came home on leave, just before Christmas. I think we were trying to cover all options. If something happened to May, he wanted me not to be alone but to have my son with me to help us look forward and not backwards.

The journey home was uneventful, and we were back in Tadworth Court, where, I have to say, they were all pleasantly surprised at the change in May. She had put on weight and was a good colour and in better health than they could ever have expected. Now it was time to go home to Scotland, but first they would just get her checked out and see how her lungs were and readjust her drugs.

Chapter 25

Scotland and Changes to Our Lives

I was going to stay with my mum and dad until I could buy a house that was suitable for us. That was no problem; they would have all of us, baby and all if we wanted. At first I had thought of going to stay with my mother-in-law as her flat was larger than my mum and dad's. Things had not changed for the better, and my father-in-law was now away from the house. I decided it was not the place to take May home to. She needed laughter and love in equal measure. Not gloom and doom. Alex agreed with me that it wouldn't work out. I don't know what reason Alex gave to his mum, if any. I may be wrong, but I don't think she was bothered, as May was another sympathy-getter. I mean, Granny got sympathy from everyone who knew her or even came in contact with her because of Dad, and May, too, was getting it for another reason. I may be wrong, but I am pretty sure I am not.

Once all was settled, the pair of us left Tadworh Court for the last time. She was never back to see them there or at Great Ormand Street, but I never forgot the kindness, the love, and the laughter that they brought into my life. When I arrived in London, I was at the lowest point in my life, and they gradually brought me, as well as my lovely little daughter, back to life again. Edna and Peter remained friends for the rest of their lives and visited us in Scotland, and, of course, we saw them when we passed through Heathrow on our travels. I could never thank them enough for what they did for all of us; they took us all into their family when they did not even know what I was like.

After all the goodbyes and best of lucks and a few tears all round, we were on the plane to Edinburgh. May and I were going home to Scotland to see Granny and Grandpa. They hadn't seen her for one and a half years. She was two years and three months when we left, and now she was three years and nine months. She had been near to heaven's door and through hell and back since then, and I with her.

We got a train in Edinburgh to Dundee, and my dad and mum were at the station to meet us. We were tired but happy to get home at last. They had everything ready for my homecoming. I had the larger of the two bedrooms, and I had sent money to buy a single bed for May, which was in place. We settled into a routine, and May continued to gain weight and was spoiled by both her grandparents. Granny Moray came to visit on her day off, so she saw her nearly every week.

Not long after we came home, a letter arrived from the Sick Children's Hospital in Edinburgh. We had an appointment to meet the paediatrician who was in charge of the CF children. He was a lovely person, quite young and devoted to his job. What a position he was in, knowing that there was no chance of his patients living into adulthood. In fact, at that time, very few of them reached school age. We met the physiotherapist who would oversee May. Everyone was very pleased with her, and I left feeling much happier. I knew that it wasn't Great Ormand Street, but they all seemed to know what they were doing. I had an appointment in two months' time and a phone number to phone if ever I was worried or felt May was unwell. She would be taken by ambulance from Dundee to the hospital, and I was not to worry—easier said than done.

We had a lovely summer that year. My dad was still working as a manager in Draffens Hairdressing Salon. The 'largest store in Scotland, north of the River Forth' was how Draffens was described. It was a lovely shop, in the style of Harrods in London and Jenners in Edinburgh. When my dad took over the department, he had taken the opportunity to visit London, going on a number of occasions to different hair conventions and business conferences. He came back every time with lots of ideas. One was to expand the Hairdressing section and make the first open salon in Dundee. On one floor you had an area with cubicles for each lady all beautifully panelled, which had not changed since the department had been opened many years before. My dad was allowed to extend to the floor above, which meant the building of a new internal stair, and there they made the most fashionable open salon to attract the young clientele. One of the male hairdressing assistants went on to be the owner of a most successful open salon of his own a few years later.

We spent a lot of weekends looking at houses. My godmother was a doctor, and I was named after her. She recommended the Valley of Strathmore or, in fact, the small towns that lay on the hillsides of the valley. I had been told in London to stay away from the coast and try to get a house inland. The doctor recommended Kirriemuir as she had always spent two weeks every year there in the past. The towns of Forfar, Kirriemuir, Alyth, Couper Angus, and Blairgowrie were the areas where our search took place. We saw houses of every shape and size—some lovely, some horrid, some you could walk into, and some so dilapidated that you would have spent a fortune just making it habitable. We saw three houses that fitted the bill; the first one was in Alyth and was part of a large Victorian mansion house. It had been divided by a builder and was in a walk-in condition. My solicitor was not happy about the communal driveway which led to a barn conversion adjacent to the main house. It was on a slope and was not in good condition as it was the original driveway. I thought long and hard about it, but I felt that Alyth was just too far out of the way from Dundee. I then looked at a property in Northmuir of Kirriemuir. It required modernisation. The bathroom was very antiquated and the kitchen non-existent. There was a huge wash house attached to the back but only a scullery in the house. I got in a builder to see how he could make a kitchen for me out of the wash house. It was already accessed from the back room of the house. He was very enthusiastic and measured it all up and thought I could have a lovely kitchen and even room to put in a table and chairs. In fact, he liked the idea so much that he bought the property himself. My solicitor was annoyed as he himself had asked the builder to come to the house. I was not all that upset as I wasn't sure about living in Northmuir. At that time, it stood alone and there were fields between it and Kirriemuir town. The brae was very steep, and I wasn't sure if May would manage it. I also had to think about myself trying to push a pram up the brae. The next property was nearer the centre of the town, and I fell in love with it. It was a semi-detached Edwardian villa. A one and a half storey they call it, when the bedrooms are built into the eaves of the house. The rooms were large with two public and two bedrooms downstairs and two large bedrooms upstairs. A kitchen was built at the back of the house, and there was a lovely bathroom downstairs and a toilet upstairs. It had hardly been touched in any way since it was built, but the bathroom was modern and the kitchen, though small, was beautifully fitted with cupboards on a wall and to the floor level. I felt at home in it whenever I went in. I could walk into it without having to do anything but give it a good clean. It had been kept in good order. It had been built by two partners in a local business, Painters and Decorators, in town—Barrie and Guild. The two houses were identical in appearance from the outside. The families of these men still lived in the houses until the death of the lady who owned the one I was looking at. I decided that this one was for me. The garden was all walled-in and private. It was surrounded by fields. It was ideal. All I had to do was buy it, and I did. St Colms, Glengate, Kirriemuir became our home in September 1967.

The weather that summer of 1967 seemed to be good. At least we were able to visit St Andrews and go on the beach quite a few times. My dad had cousins in St Andrews, and we visited them regularly. Sometimes we took a picnic and spent time on the beach in the morning and then had afternoon tea with Mary and Lizbeth, sand and all. We also began to take life as it came. Although May kept very well, there was no way we would go anywhere if the weather was cold, windy, or rainy. We learnt not to plan too far ahead and definitely not to tell anyone we would visit just in case we were unable to go. This was something that happened for the rest of her life. Some people just didn't realise how precarious May's hold on life was. They were the ones who got upset when you didn't accept their invitation to go a week later. They would exclaim 'but we are giving you a weeks' notice'. Once or twice we met my brother, Alice, and John for a day in St Andrews. One of May's favourite times was going to Camperdown Park in Dundee and getting to ride on the donkeys. How she loved it, and my dad was so proud of her, the way she sat up straight. They were happy times, and May and I enjoyed ourselves and my dad adored her.

We were due to move into our new home at the end of September. I had to organise getting all the furniture out of storage. I had arranged for some of the carpeting to be left as it was in good condition, and I knew I had carpeting in the store that would be ideal for the hall. My brother had said he would come up the day I got the keys, and as he had a car, it would be easy travelling up and down to Kirriemuir. He would stay for a couple of days until all was in place. I couldn't leave May for any length of time as neither my mum nor dad was able to do her therapy.

Leaving Tadworth Court for the last time, going home to Scotland

4th Birthday Party, with Grannies

On St Andrews beach with mummy
& granny August 1967

Chapter 26

The Gift of a Son

I had a letter from the adoption society and I was told the wonderful news that a little boy was waiting to meet his mummy. I was to phone the society to make all the arrangements. The secretary, Mrs Cunningham, would bring him up by train and would return on the overnight sleeper. My life was complete when my beautiful baby son arrived. He was not so small for six weeks—9lb; he was blond, had blue eyes, and I just adored him. To say that May was besotted is to put it mildly. My mum had a beautiful Scottish high tea all ready when Mrs Cunningham arrived, and when all the excitement had calmed down we all sat round the table.

How can I put into words what it meant to me? To be given the gift of my son, our son, May's wee brother. Andrew Moray was the future for Alex and me, the reason for having a home in Scotland and Alex working in Iran so we could give him all the chances in life we wanted him to have. We could plan for his future. He was there to be loved with all our hearts, with every bone in our body. All I wanted to do was sit and cuddle him. I knew we didn't know at that time when we would all return to Iran and be a family. It didn't matter as when Alex came home, we would be a happy family together with a future. Before that day, I never looked past the next few days because I never knew how May would be. Now we could talk about Andrew going to school like every other parent and build for his future.

Life was hectic with May to look after and my new son to take care of and love. When May was born, we were a couple with little money and had been very lucky in getting a pram from my mum and dad and a cot/bed from the Morays. This time he had the most expensive coach pram. I had a lovely time buying all the baby clothes and everything he needed without thinking of the cost. He was to get only the best. My mum and dad were wonderful;

nothing was too much of a bother and they bent over backwards to help, the consequence being that we were all very happy.

In less than a week, we were moving into the house. On the day I got the keys, Patrick and I travelled to Kirriemuir. My mum had Granny Moray coming to help look after May and the baby as my dad was at work. The house was in need of a good clean; I had bought a new Hoover and we had it and all the cleaning material in the car. We set too that day and cleaned it all. I had a new storage heater installed in the lounge as the only heating in that room was a coal fire. While the electricians were installing it, the fire station siren went off and two of the men just put down their tools and ran off down the road. We watched them as the station was only about 100 yards down the road, and it wasn't very long before we heard the fire engine leaving; what a noise it made! That was when I learnt about how the fire brigade in Kirriemuir worked. The firemen all had jobs and were called 'retained firemen'. By the time we left in the late afternoon, we had worked a miracle. The place all washed and cleaned. The house was ready for the furniture etc. to arrive the next day. Even the heater was in and working in the lounge.

My dad was taking the day off to help Mum look after the children and they were to arrive, bringing the tea with them. Patrick and I were off as soon as I had done May's therapy and fed and changed Andy. He was a very good baby; he ate and slept and smiled his windy smiles. I think that as a person I was so much happier. I had never dreamt in my wildest dreams that one day I would be moving all my furniture into my home with my two lovely children with me. I had never had the courage to dream of anything. My dad couldn't stay away, so he and Mum arrived in the middle of the afternoon. He said he thought we might need a help! So he decided to bring a baby and a four-year-old with bedroom carpets being laid upstairs. Patrick had taken May's single bed to bits first thing in the morning, and we managed to get it into the car. At least May had a bed; in fact, at one point that was all that was in the house—a large bedroom and a single bed. By teatime, all the furniture had arrived from storage and was in place. My mum and I were busy making beds. Patrick was to stay the night and leave the next day to go home. While I saw to May's therapy, her granny showed her prowess at feeding Andy his bottle. It was all a new experience for her as she had fed both my brother and me. However, she had taken to it like a duck to water. Then it was teatime and bath and bed. We had quite a routine at bedtime because May had to be involved in putting Andy to bed. A lot of tucking in and a lot of talk, kisses, and singing until she was satisfied that he was OK. She was his wee mother from then on, and they adored each other. One of the sad things in life is he can't remember his time with her or how much she loved him and cared for him. He was her life from morning until night.

Just about a week after we moved in, Isabel—one of my bridesmaids, who had a baby daughter the same age as Andy—arrived for a week's stay. This always made me laugh, but, of course, I would not have ever have said anything. Her husband, Neil, was in London for training. Isabel's mother had died while I was in London. Her dad brought her to Kirriemuir as she couldn't stay on her own with her baby. Years later, when she talked about that time, it never entered her head that I was on my own when May was born and when Margaret was born. At the time she came to stay, I was on my own with May and Andy in Kirriemuir. I only saw my mum and dad when they were able to come up. My dad was working just like her dad. I do know that I was lucky and saw them as often they could come. However, I was on my own in a strange place with no friends. She had lots of friends and in-laws and relations. I must have given off the impression that I was so very organised and capable to have people thinking that I wasn't on my own.

I can tell you there were times when I was very afraid; the responsibility of May and my lovely son gave me many concerns. I can remember crying at night in bed as I was so tired. Then there would be nights when May would start to cough. Then I had to do her therapy and get her settled and hope she was going to be all right in the morning. I always had the worry there in my mind. Other nights, it would be the baby and I would end up with him in bed beside me, just to try and get some sleep. May loved the mornings when we were all in the bed together. She would sing songs to him, and I would lie quietly and relax and just feel so much love for them both. It was at times like these that I felt so blest.

One of the first things I did when I moved into my home was to register the family with the local doctors. They came to see May as they had at that time never had a CF child as a patient. I had no problems with them as they just had to prescribe the drugs as the doctors in Edinburgh had written to tell them what was required.

I went along to the doctor for myself one day as I knew Alex was coming home in the December for his leave and I wanted to go on the pill. The doctor asked me a lot of questions about why I wanted to go on the pill, and I told him that I never wanted to bring into the world another CF child. I told him that we had adopted a child and that was the way we would have our family. The doctor said that I really couldn't go on the pill for the rest of my life. They did not know how the pill would affect the users in the long term. He felt that I should discuss it with Alex and, if he agreed, I should be sterilised. If I could let him know what Alex felt about this as soon as I could he would arrange it to be done while Alex was on leave. Alex had to sign giving his permission! How things changed in the intervening years.

We had a very exciting time at the end of November and one of the reasons for coming home. Helen was marrying Paul, and May was asked to be a flower girl. Like all little girls, she loved the getting dressed up and taking part in a wedding! We had all the fittings for the dress and I made a white fur cape lined with white satin to wear before and after the ceremony. Her dress was a deep turquoise with matching shoes and a swansdown ball for a headdress. On that day, Granny and Grandpa looked after Andy and brought him to the church so they could see her going into church then into the reception. We went to Helen's mum's house to get dressed, and her mum was quite amazed that I did not have layers upon layers of clothes to put on her in case she got cold. However, I felt that a woollen vest and a full underskirt was enough. CF children sweat a lot, and if she started to overheat and sweat and then cooled down, she would be wearing damp underwear. I understood Helen's mum being overprotective as she had lost a little girl who was two years old and suffered from Down's syndrome and a heart condition and was a very sickly little child.

What a great day May had! She was very well behaved in church, and at the reception, she was up dancing and playing with a little boy guest. No one in the room would have known that she was anything but a normal little four-year-old. What a happy day we had!

The nearer it got to Christmas, the more the excitement rose. Daddy was coming home for Christmas. I wondered how Alex would feel. How my life had changed in the last two years! Gone was the little wife who let her husband decide what was to happen—buying a house without my seeing it beforehand and selling the same house and arranging for it to be emptied without any input from me. Contacting the company to get all the travel arrangements seen to for us to come out, arranging the doctor's appointments for our injections and for May's care in Iran. You name it, he did it. Now I did everything for myself. I did not require any help with anything. I was independent; it was now my turn to buy a home, and most of all, bring into his home our son. Just what would he think of it all?

All this time, Granny Moray would come up on a Saturday evening and go home on a Sunday. All her conversation was about herself and the position she was in. I don't think she ever really took in how ill May was. Even though she did not look as if there was anything wrong with her, she was a very sick little girl. We all knew she was on borrowed time, but I am sure Granny Moray never got her head around it. As for Andrew, well, she seemed to take him for granted. Sometimes Andy brought her up and came for her. She cried a lot, and I noticed that May was wetting the bed when she came to stay. I told the doctor about it and he was very sure that Granny Moray was the cause. He said that I had to tell my mother-in-law to stop crying in front of May or not visit. I wasn't as blunt as he was, but I did tell her the first time she worked herself into a weep to please not to do it in front of May as she became very upset on seeing her crying. It wasn't good for her and we all wanted her to be happy. Well, she stopped it during the day, but when we were sitting after the pair were in their beds, she always got round to the subject and the tears would fall. I am afraid, my mum and dad had little or no time for her. They thought that she was self-centred and blinkered to all but herself. I had, of course, an added worry during this time as it would be quite a while before Andrew's adoption could be finalised as Alex had to spend a month with him, and I was afraid something would happen and he would be taken from us.

By the time Alex was due home, I had a date for the hospital, Forfar Infirmary, for my sterilisation. We also had the date for the house visit for the courts, and my solicitor was all geared up to make sure that the adoption got through as soon as possible. All I had to do was be at the window with May and Andy, waiting for my dad to bring Alex from the station in Dundee. Every time Alex came home, wherever we were, it was exciting for both of us. He couldn't wait to be with me again and I with him. This time was so special as he would see his new baby son for the first time, and May. As he said, 'being with her was a bonus'. I always felt that he worried he would never see her again. He loved his son on sight, and he was such a lovely baby and so good. He also loved his house. I had sent out pictures before I had bought it, but they didn't do it justice. May took him round the house, into every room and cupboard, and told him all about them—whose room it was and, lastly, where he was to sleep. She said that he wasn't to be frightened because she was just across the hall from him. It was a hectic leave—firstly Christmas, my mum and dad on Christmas Eve through Christmas Day, and Granny Moray on Boxing Day. She always went to Alex's at Christmas. Alex took my mum and dad home on the morning of Boxing Day as he was getting my dad's car to collect his mum and bring her up to Kirriemuir. He took her home on the twenty-seventh, and then he went for my mum and dad again and they stayed until after New Year. We had a very happy time. Then I was in hospital, and, would you believe it, the court sent their representative to visit while I was there. He happened to be one of the Kirriemuir solicitors, a Mr Donaldson. My mum and dad had come to help Alex with the children. Alex had to do her physiotherapy for the first time; he said he was so afraid in case he hurt her. Alex was visiting me when Mr Donaldson arrived at the house. May, of course, was with her granny when she opened the door to him. After all the introductions, he looked in the pram to see her baby brother, whom she introduced to him with his full name. She then took over, and my mum says she just let her as we couldn't have had a better ambassador than her. She was such a taking little girl and so polite. She showed Mr Donaldson Andy's bedroom and told him that Andy was too small to be in it yet, but he would go into it when he was bigger. She said that her daddy had a 'baby listener' already fitted. Did he know what that was? Of course, she didn't let him answer, she just told him 'it was so Mummy and Daddy can hear if he cries as you don't want him to be upset. They can run upstairs and pick him up and cuddle him'. She took him into every room and showed him her bedroom last. She even explained why she had a tent over her bed. My mum made a cup of tea, and they sat in the lounge and partook of the feast. When Mr Donaldson was leaving, he told her that he was going to see her daddy and mummy in hospital. My mum said that she and Dad were flabbergasted when she said, 'Will you tell the man in the court that we can keep my baby as we don't want him taken away?'

He reassured her, saying that she and her baby brother 'were very lucky to live in such a lovely house with lots of love in it'. My mum told us later that the look of amazement on his face when he looked at my mum was something to see.

We had the meeting in a small room in the hospital. Mr Donaldson said that his meeting us was a privilege and he would do everything in his power to smooth the way. There was no doubt how much both the children were loved by the entire household.

Once I was home, again life went back to our usual routine. May took up a large part of the day with her therapy, but Andy didn't miss out on his time. May played with him and spent all her time mothering him. We visited the hospital in Edinburgh and the doctor there was very pleased and said that he saw no reason why, if things did not change, we could not go out to Abadan.

Alex told me when he came home that the Mashar houses had been condemned—surprise, surprise—and everyone was now living in Abadan. Alex was due back the middle of February, although I and the children could not leave the country until after the adoption took place. The doctor said he would have all the drugs required for a stay of eight to nine months and worked out that it would cost us about £400 if we did not get them on the NHS. However, he said that he would do what he could to get it for us free. We felt that no matter how much it cost we would pay. We already had a humidifier in Iran. So everything was settled that after Andrew's adoption went through and she had the OK from the doctor, I would go out to Iran. Too soon Alex left again, but with a lot to look forward to and so many happy memories of his leave. It could be less than a month before we were with him. He said I would like my house in Abadan, he was sure, and all the ladies from Mashar were my neighbours.

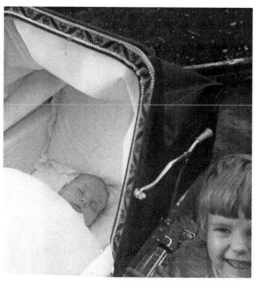

May and Andrew aged 6 weeks.
September 1967

Flower girl at special 'Aunties'
Wedding Nov 1967

With mummy outside the church.
Nov 1967

Posing on her own-Nov 1967

Dancing the night away with new friend. Nov 1967

With granny and grandad, last night before returning to Iran 1968

Chapter 27

Back to Iran, 1968

Alex had just left, when I got a phone call from my solicitor to tell me that Andrew's adoption had gone through and he was lawfully ours. I dashed through to where he was sitting with May, lifted him up, and danced and skipped about the house singing 'you're mine, you're mine'. May sang and danced with me, and I hugged her and hugged him and we were so happy. I telephoned my dad and he said, 'We will be up to see you. I am having the afternoon off.' So they came up, and my dad just lifted him up in his arms and I could see Dad was crying. I just realised that my dad had never touched him until that day. Oh, he had cooed and laughed at him, but he had never touched him. He was afraid that something would happen and we wouldn't get to keep him. I did not say anything, but I was nearly in tears myself. He recovered, and from that moment on, Andy and he were inseparable. When I look back on that time until I left to go to Abadan, I remember how my dad showed my children so much love. He did not have good health and was just about to retire in the June. It was as if he wanted to pour his love out to them to make up for the months without them.

May and I went to the hospital in Edinburgh for her last check-up, and I collected a box of drugs costing over £400. The down payment on our house was £700, so that tells you just what the value of these drugs was. All that, of course, was immaterial as we never took anything like that into consideration. She required the drugs, so we got them. Our tickets arrived, and before we knew it, we were off to Abadan. We had three cases of clothes, an overnight bag with the drugs required for the journey, and all the nappies and bottles and everything that I would require for an overnight stay in a Heathrow Airport Hotel and a seven-hour flight. The rest of the drugs were discreetly placed in the main cases. I will always remember that flight because May had her own flight bag with her nightdress and change of clothes for the next day and she wanted to show the air stewardess what she thought was a lovely nightdress—not once but on three flights by the time we got to Abadan. Why, I don't know; maybe it was a throwback from all the months of wearing horrible hospital clothes.

We had to get off the plane at Beruit and change to the flight to Abadan. The planes were always comfortable, and at that time, airlines always asked families with children to go on board first. This meant you weren't being hassled and the stewardess helped you on board. I had the front seat with a sky cot on a bench in front us. May always enjoyed her flights, and Andy slept most of the way. He was seven months old, and May was four years and seven months old. When I hear women and men say their children are too young to fly and they couldn't be bothered with all the hassle etc., etc. I just wonder what they are talking about when I look back at my experiences and those of other mothers like me who were away for anything up to a year. The worst part of the journey was getting from Kirriemuir to London. It took longer for that part than it did to fly from London to Abadan. It wasn't just the journey but the whole package—the entire luggage that we required for our stay; it is not easy when there is a seven-month-old baby, growing all the time, who would be sixteen months by the time we came home again.

The journey, well, we had to take a car journey from Kirriemuir to Dundee, then a rail journey to Edinburgh, then a taxi to Edinburgh Airport, and, lastly, a flight to London. The luggage was booked in from Edinburgh to Abadan. Once we landed at Heathrow, things were much better. I just had my hand luggage, and I put the baby in a trolley. We looked for the bus with our hotel name on it somewhere at the Arrivals door and got on the bus. They took us to our hotel for the night and brought us back the next day.

You must also remember that during the journey, I had to make sure that May got her therapy and Andy had to be fed and changed; there were no disposable nappies. Then the next worst part of that journey was arriving in Abadan and the usual melee at the customs. However, we did enjoy the flights; they were great. You have to remember I had to take everything for our stay—I was leaving United Kingdom in the winter and would be arriving in United Kingdom in the winter, but there would be a very hot summer in between.

Alex was waiting for us with Peter and Gill, and off we went in a taxi to our new home in South Bawarda, the other end of Abadan from the airport. In fact, it was the other end from everything except the Taj Cinema. My neighbours were Iranian families, and I did not see very much of them at all—just said hello in the passing. I was, however, surrounded by most of the tug staff that came from Bander Mashar and a number of those who had lived in Abadan for a number of years. I missed John and Shona as they were further away in another cluster of tug staff homes, further in Bawarda.

The houses were made of concrete blocks and had flat roofs, which were periodically covered with a new layer of straw and mud to help keep them cool. They had been up since the late 1940s as some of the tug staff were evacuated in 1951 from the same area at the time when Mosaddeq nationalised the oil holdings. There was a patio area at the entrance to the house which was at the side of the house. It was half the breadth of the house. The other half was a part of the house which stuck out from the entrance wall. When you came in through the front door you were faced with a long hallway. On the left was a bedroom which was in the bit that was jutting out and made up one side of the patio. Next to that room was a large bathroom; the next room was the dining room with a door off to the kitchen. From the front door, the first door on the right-hand side led to a large bedroom, and facing you at the end of the hallway was the door into the lounge. These two rooms faced the front garden. The lounge was large and had a door leading into the kitchen. The whole house was tiled all through with a bit of a mixture of coloured tiles. I will say that they were all the same colour but different shades, so they really did look odd. The walls were all a dull pale green as far as I can remember—most were the same colour—and the ceiling was high. All my furniture from Mashar was there plus a round table with a large brass plate inserted into the top. It was a lovely piece of furniture. One of Alex's friends, Bob Ray, had gifted it to him when they left Mashar. He was going into bachelor accommodation, and there was no room for it as the flats were bedsitters. My carpets looked better in this house than they did in Mashar. However, the windows, although they appeared to be big, weren't so and it was quite dark, just as it was in Mashar. A door from the kitchen led into a back compound enclosed by high walls on the right to my neighbour and on the left to my driveway. The bottom wall was made up of Jabber's room and toilet and a storeroom.

Once we had visited the hospital with May to sort out her treatment and confirmed the arrangement should we require them, life got into its own pace. It didn't change, no matter where I lived, Scotland or Iran. My first priority was May and Andy. Jabber, of course, was very pleased to see me and was over the moon with the baby. He had four daughters and no sons. He was worried about his old age as the boys in the family always looked after the parents as they got older. There was no retirement pension for the people in Iran. I saw the girls quite often but never his wife at that time. The girls were all in school and so were in European clothes. They were very olive-skinned but nice-looking girls.

One of my main aims all through May's life, when not in hospital, was to try to make it appear as normal as I could. You have to remember that May very often had difficulty getting her breath and sometimes her cough was very distressing, and both were extremely tiring. Whether she had a good day or a bad day, her therapy and her antibiotics and her diet and her supplementary pills went on 24-7 without a break. Our life revolved around her, but we tried to make the rest of the days as good as we could. Now with a baby as well, I did not have many moments to myself, but I was so happy to be out with Alex and the children. I thanked God for giving me this time and hoped we could be together for a while. The next big day of our life was Andy's christening. The new minister for St Christopher's Church had just arrived before us. His first service was to be Andy's christening. He came to see us, and we found him extremely nice. He was a young married man, an American, and we just clicked with him. It was quite an evening not only for us, but also for him. There was to be a party at our house after the service. That was a bit of a headache for me as I had no idea what to serve. However, I managed with a cold buffet. Alex and I went to the bazaar and bought ham and salad food. Then we went to the Staff Store, where I bought all the other ingredients. I made pastry and made sausage rolls. Jabber put on a curry and rice for those who wanted it. I had nibbles out of the Staff Store and crisps and nuts from the bazaar to have in bowls around the lounge to eat when we came in, as we were going to toast my lovely son. The service was very nice. Nell Richards, from our Bandar Mashar days, carried Andy into the church, and Alex's friend Bob was the godfather. Nell and I returned home; Nell got Andy bathed and into his sleep suit. I always thought he looked like Andy Pandy from the TV. My job was to give May her therapy. She was full of talk of the church and putting the water on her brother's head. She didn't like that. Once she was ready for bed, we let them stay up until everyone arrived from the church. This was my first party in Abadan, and I have to say it bore no resemblance to any I had at home. We had one of the engineers with his accordion. One of the women had a lovely voice, so she sang and the drink flowed. The taped music had some up dancing, and still the drink flowed. I do not know what time we went to bed in the early hours of the morning. I was very tired that Monday, but I had to manage both May and Andy as Alex was away to work. The wonderful thing about having a houseboy was there was no mess. When I got up to see to Andy, the house looked as if it had never had a large party going on in it a few hours earlier.

Life was good; the children and I went to various houses to visit regularly. One house in particular was of Ruth Shaw, whom we knew from Mashar. We all congregated there about eleven o'clock for morning coffee and stayed there until about 1 p.m., when we all departed home for lunch. Then it was siesta time in the afternoon. Then around 4 p.m., some of the other children would come round to play with May, or I would play with her in the garden, or we would go for a walk. If Alex wasn't at home, I would just have my tea with the children, and then it would be bath and bed. In between all this, I had to do May's therapy. I was managing her diet; it was limited because of no fat—when she had bacon and egg, it was grilled bacon and a poached egg; she had fish fingers with potato cake and peas. She could not have chips. Mince and potatoes with vegetables mixed in was a favourite, and, of course, Andy ate what she ate as there was no baby food. I went down to the fish bazaar if Alex was at home, and I came home with a red snapper. I filleted it and cut it into meal-sized pieces, and for Alex and me, I dipped it into a batter and did it in deep fat, along with chips. I did it in breadcrumbs or in a white sauce for the children. I cut it into fish-finger sizes as they liked fish fingers, and I cooked these in the oven. I sometimes went to the meat bazaar, and I would come home with the backbone of a lamb amongst my buys. They were all chopped for me by the man in the bazaar. I made the most wonderful lamb stews with lots of fresh vegetables from the bazaar too. The only thing was they were so small it took a whole back to make a stew for all of us. Even May got that. I used to leave the stew to cool and skimmed the fat from the top before adding the vegetables and returning the dish to the oven. Lastly, when it was cooked, I added gravy browning or Oxo, depending on what I could get my hands on. As May loved chicken, we had it in all different ways imaginable from roast to chicken rissoles. I would say that 90 per cent of all the food we ate was made from scratch. The one thing I was still not good at was making bread, but I did eventually learn even that. I found it a bit easier to feed May in Abadan as I was able to get a bit more variety. It was very important that she did not eat fat, as it passed through her, bringing all the other food with it, and that was why she had to take the pills whose contents was the 'pancreas of a boar'. However, I must have been successful as she gained weight and grew.

As the summer came in, we started to go to the pool in Bawarda, and there I met Shona and her family. It did not take Andy long to swim. In fact, he was swimming before he could walk. May enjoyed herself as she had been in a pool quite often at Tadworth, so she was used to splashing in the baby pool or sitting in the nice cool water beside me as I walked about with my hand on Andy's tummy while he did his stuff. They were really a lovely colour, but it soon became too hot to go about without having a T-Shirt on. It got to 130° in the shade. If there was a wind blowing in from the water of the Shatt Al-Arab, it would be so humid and smelly (sharshi). If it was coming from the desert, it would be dry and hot (shamal). One story that one of the women told was quite funny. There was a conversation about the weather and the heat between herself and another couple, and they described it as so hot that 'one could fry an egg on the road'. One day she found that she was short of eggs in her fridge, only to find out that her young son had taken her literally and was trying to fry eggs in the middle of the road outside the house where the tar had melted with the heat. He was, of course, unsuccessful!

One day after being at the pool, May had a temperature and was feeling sick. I phoned her doctor and he said bring her to the hospital. They had her room all set up by the time I got her there. We doubled her dose of antibiotics, giving them to her every two hours, and had her in an oxygen tent with her humidifier from her bedroom. I stayed with her and gave her extra therapy, We were very lucky as the temperature reduced and her chest did not fill up, and within two or three days, she was home. She was a bit peaky, but at least we had saved her from pneumonia, which, I knew, could kill her. However, that was the end of her visits to the pool and in consequence unless Alex took him, Andy's as well. The doctor said there was far too great a risk of infection from the pool, and I, for one, was not going to risk it. Once again I had been reminded that May was a sick child with an incurable illness, and I must never take her life for granted.

One of the changes I noticed between Bander Mashar and Abadan was in the tug staff. When we were in Bander Mashar, I had found everyone very friendly. You mixed with everyone. There were a few tug staff who did keep themselves to themselves, but the majority could be found at anything that was happening. I soon realised that in Abadan, the senior staff lived in Braim, except for Fred Richards, who lived round the corner from our house. The rest of the married tug staff lived in Bawarda, one or two in North Bawarda, but the rest in South Bawarda. Of course, Abadan was a large town. It was built round its refinery, which was, at one time, the largest in the world. The airport and the Golf Club were on the west side of the town, off the Khorramashahr Road. Khorramashahr was the port for everything but oil, and although I am not sure how far away it was, I think it may have been ten miles up the river. Braim housing, the bachelor flats, and the hotel were all in the same area of the town. The hospital was adjacent to the refinery on that side of the town. You had to travel all the way around the refinery to get to Bawarda. South Bawarda housing was built parallel to the river up to the point where the tank farm for the refinery started, but it went some distance inland and was quite large. It was the original housing and had been up pre-1950. Alex and I had a quiet kind of social life at that time, due to May and her condition. If we could not go out with her, we very rarely went out in the evening unless it was to visit around the doors. Alex was on a day shift at this time so he worked Saturday to Thursday.

This was the first time I came across the 'oil and water' in the tug staff. I noticed it the first time I went to the pool. There was a clique who always sat together, like some exclusive club. It was always the same lot together, all laughing at their 'in' jokes. I was surprised at first as they were all tug captains. They were young, quite loud, and typical English abroad. It was, to my eyes, not quite the thing. I was surprised that Shona and John could be found with them. Everywhere you went, if they happened to be there as well, their group would be all together, always a bit apart. I began to think that they really thought they were superior to the rest of us. Some, I have to say, were worse than others, and I used to say to Alex that if we were at home, I wouldn't give some of them houseroom. Alex and I were too busy with our own life to join any group, but if we did have a group, it was within the Golf Club. On Fridays, Alex went golfing with the Engineering Superintendent, who was his boss. Also in the group were the bachelor engineers. 'The three musketeers' I called them. I would go to the club by taxi to meet him sometimes for a curry lunch or around 5 p.m. for tea. I would meet the superintendent's wife, who had a baby girl about Andy's age. She was American and had been a teacher in Abadan before her marriage. I also met some of the single women who taught at the school or worked in the office. Alex had bought me a set of golf clubs and a bag as one of my birthday presents. I did not use them very much at that time, although Alex arranged for me to have lessons and looked after the children when I had them. On other Fridays, we went to the Karting Club, where most of the time the owners of the carts were maintaining them and tweaking them up before the races. It was light-hearted enjoyment and a relaxing day out. I have lots of slides of Andy and May in the train that was a great delight to all the youngsters. They waited for it to come out every week. The group there were a much more mixed group, some engineers and some captains, but also a number of expatriates who worked for the oil company or its associates and some locals. I have to say that all the time I was in Iran, we never joined any particular clique; we mixed with whoever happened to be the people doing what we were doing. We had each other, and we were happy to be that way.

Around this time, Jabber brought into the house from the bazaar four little yellow chickens, which he thought would grow into hens. However, after playing with them and Daddy sitting with one on his head, it was decided that they weren't suitable. Jabber said he would take them home to his house. The next thing to arrive was a little white rabbit. We kept him, and he lived in a hutch in the house in the summer and in the compound in the winter. Then along came Tom, a small ginger kitten, who grew rapidly into a very large fluffy cat. I think Jabber just liked to give the children gifts, and these were gifts he could give them.

One incident that still sticks in my mind happened after I had been told not to take May to the pool. This is an example of the way the minds of some of people work. There was one couple, a captain and his wife, who had married later in life than the rest of us. She had been a nurse in Abadan Hospital, and they had met when he came to work in Abadan. I had met them in Mashar when I had been out there and I knew they were very quiet and did not mix as much as some of the rest of us. However, I liked her very much, and she had been to see me when I arrived in Abadan. They were very careful with their boy and girl—very protective of them and kept them in out of the sun and, in general, kept them close. After I stopped going to the pool, one of the tug staff wives came to visit me. I had had very little contact with her, but, of course, we knew each other as Alex had worked with her husband. When she came in, she wanted to know why I was not coming to the pool any more. 'I hope you are not going to be like the _____ not letting the children come out and play and not going to the pool etc.' I was very annoyed; it showed how little she understood what was wrong with May. I would have loved May to go out to play and go to the pool, but I also wanted to keep her healthy. I had no choice in the matter, and we were quite different from the other family. The more I saw of some of the expatriates, the more I realised that when you live in the environment that we were living in, you had to stay friends with people and just keep smiling, no matter how you felt. I have always remained friends with a number of them to this day, especially Shona and John; life is too short. Some of them improved as time went by, It could I suppose be put down to the freedom of being away from the restriction of life in the United Kingdom. I just felt it was an awful pity to behave as if you were somehow superior when you were a captain of a tugboat. I remember something Alex once said to me. I don't remember why, but I never forgot it. I think it might have been in connection with one captain in particular being under the influence of drink to the stage he could not work, while on duty. Alex said, 'I can berth a tanker any day, but none of them could mend an engine.' However, Alex being Alex, he had said it without malice or intent. The thing that amused me was the fact that very few of the people who had a superior notions had had the private education or life style that Alex had known. I wonder if they would have let him join if they had!

Sometimes I found the strain of the responsibility of May and Andy too much. I tried to lead a normal life, but there was nothing normal about it at all. I wanted to give Andy as much of my love and attention as I could, and, at the same time, be a nurse, physiotherapist, and dietician to May, as well, of course, as being her mummy. I was happiest when I had both of them in the house or garden on my own. We used to sit and read Nursery Rhyme Books, stories of Winnie the Poo etc. most afternoons as it was too hot outside during the summer. Andy loved to sit between us, and he used to watch us like a game of tennis, first one way then the other. I don't know how I did cope, but I somehow did. I always looked after Andy first; that was the routine I had set up at home. Once he was up, washed and dressed, and in his high chair, I fed him his breakfast—cereal with fruit or porridge. I left him with his bottle then as he got more able his cup. I would then start on May. I would give her the therapy (tips and taps, Alex used to say they were more like thumps and bumps). How long it took depended on how easy it was to remove the sticky mucus. Then she had a wash and dressed, and then we sat down for breakfast. Of course, before she ate it, she had some sixteen pills of one kind and another—a salt pill, then vitamins followed by antibiotics, and lastly some eight large pills, horse pill size, containing the 'pancreas of a boar'. I have to say in all honesty, for 90 per cent of the time she was no bother, but some days she tried to rebel but I could not give in to her. By the time breakfast was over, I would go and shower and dress myself. Then Jabber and I would spend time working out the meal for the night and I would do the day's washing. Sometimes I took the children to the Staff Store, which was a short walk away or we went visiting for a coffee. By that time it was lunchtime, and I would start May over again—therapy, a wash, then pills. We all had a snack lunch of scrambled eggs or home-made soup or something similar. Then it was time for bed for the little ones. I then saw to the evening meal if I was making something. Sometimes Jabber made the whole meal, and at other times, we would work together. It depended on what it was. He never mastered making stovies or pancakes, but he was good at other things. Then I would play with the children, and if it wasn't too hot, we would go into the garden. May had a bike with stabilisers, which she rode very well. It wasn't easy once Andy started wanting to be put down on the ground as I couldn't let him down in the garden. The garden was watered by using water from the Shatt Al-Arab and was contaminated by lots of foul unmentionables. I often just took them for a walk if May felt like it. By then it was time to start the whole process for the third time that day. By the time I had bathed Andy and had him in his sleepsuit, then May's therapy and bath and got her into her nightdress, Jabber had their tea ready. It would be what Alex and I were eating unless it was totally unsuitable. We always had child portions of cooked meat mince and cooked chicken mince in the freezer. You have to remember I could not buy baby food, and our diet was restricted to what we could buy in the Staff Store or the bazaar. Once tea was over, Daddy was usually home and he was there to put them to bed but not before May had her last therapy. If we were lucky, we would get a full night's sleep, but if it was bad, I could be up with May during the night. I was, by now, looking like a skinned rabbit. The mental and physical strain had to show somewhere. I never told Alex how I felt, and he never mentioned anything to me about how he felt. I have to say that for all the work and worry, we were a very happy family. After all, we had been told May would never live outside a hospital, and here we were a proper family.

May and Andy both had birthdays in August. She was five years old and he was one year old. We had two birthday parties, a small one for Andy and a proper one for May. The next big step and a very important one for May and us was starting school. She became a pupil in Abadan Overseas School. Our day started very early to get everything in before she left by the school bus. She was home for lunch and there was a repeat performance, then off again for the afternoon. She was home for tea, and before we knew it, it was bedtime. Of course, every time she came from school, the first thing I did was her therapy. I tried missing out the lunchtime. This seemed to work, but I didn't always feel happy about that routine. I played it a lot by ear. Andy and I had a lot more time to ourselves, and by this time, he was just about walking. He would walk around the house holding on to my hands forever and ever, but if I let go, he just plonked down on to his bottom and scuttled along on it across the tiled floors. I don't remember him ever actually crawling. He was a big boy, happy and very content with his lot. I was surprised that May got on so well at the school. I was afraid she would not manage; she never said 'I don't like it', or 'I can't manage'.

We adapted our life once again, and the new routine became the normal thing. We enjoyed ourselves as every festival from Easter in the spring to Guy Fawkes in the autumn was an excuse to have a party. If it wasn't for the children, it was for the adults. Sometimes the children's parties ended up with more adults than children. The Golf Club was a good place to have them, and Fred Richards was great at organising them.

The time was getting nearer to my returning to the United Kingdom in November. It had passed in a flash, and I was taking May home as well as she had been when I arrived. She had her last visit to the hospital for her check-up and I got a letter for the hospital in Edinburgh. The time had passed so quickly, but I was looking forward to seeing my mum and dad and my home in Scotland. Alex was due home in January, so we would not be parted so very long this time.

House in Abadan

House in Abadan

May, Mummy and brother in garden, April 1968

On bike in garden of abadan house April 1968

With her beloved brother August 1968

Chapter 28

Winter 1968

The journey home was quite interesting. When we got on the plane, a VC 10, in Abadan it was going straight to London. It stopped, but we did not have to leave the plane. I was given the seat at the front of the plane as usual with a sky cot. Well, of course, Andy had reached an age when he wasn't interested in a cot. The galley of the plane was just behind the partition in front of my seat. On board were a group of climbers who had been visiting Everest. Don't ask me how they had got from Everest to Abadan as I do not know. My only guess was that they flew from Nepal to Karachi in Pakistan to Abadan. Within minutes of the plane being airborne, they were up in the galley, looking for—yes, you have guessed—beer or, even better, a little spirits. I had to keep rescuing Andy from under their feet. May called them 'these great big hairy monsters'. However, it didn't take either of them long before they were both being made of. My biggest worry was trying to stop Andy from being trampled upon as they progressively became more and more under the weather. I kept being told they hadn't had a drink for four months or something like that. I nearly said, 'Well you don't have to drink a whole four months' in one go'. Also, of course, it was the days of cigarettes, and what with the smell from their clothes and the smoke, well, it wasn't all that pleasant.

We did our usual when we got to London; we had a night in a hotel. Andy was wide awake when we landed, but immediately we got on the hotel bus, he just went out like a light. A heavyweight at any time, he was so much heavier when asleep. We were up at the crack of dawn to get ready for our flight up to Scotland. We took a train to Dundee, and there was Grandpa waiting for us. Granny was in Kirriemuir, getting everything ready for our homecoming.

Once we were settled at home, I phoned Edinburgh to the Sick Children's Hospital and was given an appointment to see May's doctor. They were very pleased with her and thought she should start school after the Christmas holidays. We then visited the doctor's surgery in Kirriemuir. They spoke about her going to the school in Dundee for children with special needs. I explained that I was not going to send her there. She was able to go to a normal school. She did not have anything wrong with her brain or her body. Her illness was medical, and with the help and understanding of the school, she would be all right. It was decided that she would not go while the weather was bad, but maybe after Easter. I decided to go along to the school and speak to the headmaster about her attending. Reform Street Primary School was an old Victorian building right in the centre of Kirriemuir. It was not a long walk from the house, probably five minutes' slow walk, and ideal for us. I took May down with me when I went, and Mr Black was very nice. He told her all about the school badge, which was Peter Pan, and asked her if she had heard of him. She was able to say that she had a book at home which had pictures of Peter Pan, Captain Hook, and a fairy called Tinkle Bell. He said he looked forward to her coming to the school, whenever the doctors let her come. She was quiet about it, but when she got home, she told Granny and Grandpa all about it.

With May not going to school, we settled once again into a routine which suited our lifestyle. Granny Moray came up on a Saturday to visit about once a fortnight, and my mum and dad visited as often as they could. Dad had retired in June 1968, so they were free to visit when they wanted to. He kept the garden, and my mum loved nothing better than hanging out the washing and ironing it and having it all in a neat pile to use. She was also happy in the kitchen. I managed very well as May was really keeping much better and even the journey home had not bothered her. We kept up her reading and her writing every day, and we did crafts and drew pictures for Granny and Grandpa.

The time went by very quickly, and with the run-up to Christmas and then Daddy to look forward to, we were never weary. Christmas was as usual; Mum and Dad came up a few days before, and Granny Moray came up over the New Year. She wasn't any better than before I went to Iran; however, I just didn't take her on at all. She kept telling me that 'they had never had anything like May's illness in their family'. She was determined not to understand what was wrong with May and that it was because we both carried the recessive gene. Her main topic of conversation was my father—in-law. She wanted him back! Why, I have no idea as she couldn't say a good word about him.

Alex came home in January, and we had a very quiet leave during the week. Then, at weekends, we seemed to have friends with family every weekend. Friends came from Dundee one weekend, Arbroath family another, my brother and family and Andy with his family of two girls. I enjoyed this very much, even though it was tiring. We could not guarantee that May would be able to visit, so it suited us very well. We had the room, so why not. We did go out to visit in the afternoon sometimes, and that was a change. However, I did not like going out for meals with May. I could not give her the therapy properly, and she had to take so many pills and potions. We could not stay away as she slept in her tent and was fed glycol through her humidifier. It didn't bother me; I just wanted her to be well and for all of us to be happy.

She attended Edinburgh Sick Kids every month and always had therapy there. Sometimes I felt that her nose was a bit stuffed up. The doctor felt that her sinuses could do with cleaning out. He would see about it before we went away again to Daddy.

Too soon, Alex's leave was over, and he was off again in March. It was better now as we knew we would be out to see him probably in June. One of the tug staff was retiring, and as he had a larger house with air conditioning in the dining room—which meant you could use it as a bedroom when the children were older—Alex had applied for it. It was on the same road as the house we were in, but at the other side of the main road that dissected the housing area. It was the first house on the corner and behind it was the Staff Store. Alex said that I could walk out of my back garden gate and be at the back of the store. We would wait until he had moved in before we came out. It was nice to be thinking forward as we very rarely did that, at least not months away.

May was starting school, so I went down to see the headmaster just before Easter break to tell him that the doctors were pleased for her to start after the Easter Holidays. He welcomed her with a very cheery hello on the day she was to start and took her along to the classroom. He knocked on the door and went in. We stood just inside the door, waiting. The next thing I knew, the teacher, an elderly woman, turned to Mr Black and told him very loudly that she wasn't 'having that child in her classroom'. She said, 'She should be at a special school. She would need special attention, and she didn't have time to put her coat on and look after her needs.'

I couldn't believe what I was hearing; I was absolutely shocked. I said, 'My daughter doesn't need anything from you but understanding. She is probably more capable of looking after herself than any other child in your classroom. She won't need you to "put on her coat".' I can't tell you all that was said, but one thing that was said has stuck out in my mind ever since. 'If that child comes into my classroom, I leave.'

I began to walk out; I was nearly in tears, and this was an awful type of discrimination. Another reason I was upset was that May was standing there, listening to all that was being said. Since going to school in Abadan, she had begun to realise that other children didn't eat lots of pills or have physiotherapy three or four times a day. They didn't cough like she did or get breathless when they ran about like she did sometimes. In fact, she was beginning to realise she was different. She was nearly six years old and a bright, intelligent little girl. Mr Black said how sorry he was, but I felt that May and I should never have been in the position he placed us in. It should have all been sorted out before we went to the school. He must have known what was going to happen.

I walked home, the anger in me boiling up, the nearer I got to the house. I immediately looked up the Education Department for Tayside and got the number of the Head of the Department. I phoned him up, and he answered straight away. I told him my name and that I was phoning from Kirriemuir.

Before I said any more he replied, 'Mrs Moray, I am so sorry about what happened this morning. Mr Younger of Webster Seminary will take May after the holidays with great pleasure. Please accept our apologies. It should never have happened.'

Mr Black must have telephoned right after I left, and Mr Robertson had contacted Mr Younger and that was that. However, I explained that the school was at the other side of town. It had two braes between us and the school. No matter which route we took, it was not going to be so easy for us as going to Reform Street. He could do nothing about that; I could not even get a school bus which passed my door to stop and pick her up as we lived within the three-mile limit.

After Easter, she started at Webster Seminary, primary department, and they were very nice. Going to school in the morning and coming home in the evening was not a problem; the big problem was lunchtime. I had to walk over for her, down a steep brae and up a steep brae, and then walk the incline of the Glengate to nearly the top, where we lived. Therapy, lunch, and then the return journey, all in an hour. If my mum and dad were staying, my dad picked her up at lunchtime and brought her home. It was still a rush, and it was doing no good to her or to me. After we had tried it for a couple weeks, I decided to ask if she could stay for school lunch. If I gave the school her pills, would the school nurse give her the eight she required at lunchtime? I would give them enough for five days in boxes, one box for each day. 'Of course, we will do that,' they said. Now I felt we were getting somewhere. As she wasn't to get her therapy at lunchtimes, I would do it whenever she got in and again before her tea.

One lovely little story came about at that time. When I collected her one day from school, she informed me that the school dentist was coming the next day. Her teeth were very discoloured with all the drugs she took, and until all her second teeth came through we were struggling with the baby ones. I told her, 'Just tell him you take lots of medicines which have coloured your teeth.' She thought about it for a minute or two and seemed to be quite happy about what to say. When I collected her the next day I asked her how she had got on with the dentist.

'Fine' was the reply. 'I just told him I was on drugs and he said to me, "Well, don't tell your mum," but I told him you knew.' That was our May, serious little soul. I often wondered if the dentist kept a straight face.

One day, we were in the lovely park in Kirriemuir called the Den. We lived very near to it, and I took the children down there to play on the swings and use the chute. I met the mother of a little girl in May's class, who had told her that May had been crying that day. When I got home, I tried to find out what was happening. I realised that she was not getting her pills at lunchtime and she was not as happy as I had thought she was. I had asked very little of the school—the pills and also if they could they keep her in if it was raining. I always got the same answer, 'Of course, Mrs Moray, no bother'. It just so happened that she had to visit Edinburgh for her monthly check up, and Dr Adams wasn't as happy with her as he had been before.

He said, 'Nothing to worry about but maybe a week off school would not go amiss.' He wanted her in a week hence to have her sinuses cleaned anyway. Just give her a wee rest before the operation. I was quite happy to keep her off school as I was beginning to worry about it anyway. I was now anxious to get her out to Abadan; life was so much easier out there. I was on my own in Kirriemuir, so getting up in the night was not good. I was finding the broken nights difficult, and then I had to get May up in time for school and then cope with a toddler. No Daddy and no Jabber to help.

It was the beginning of June and Alex wrote to say the house was just about ready; it had been painted inside as it was all a bit grubby when the furniture had been removed by the last occupants. Whenever May came out of hospital, I was to phone up Rank and Khun, the travel agents, and see about the tickets and visas. I couldn't wait; it was hard to believe that life in Abadan was easier, but the hospital, the school, the teachers, and our friends were so supportive. I found that life in Scotland with a child with cystic fibrosis was no picnic. There was no help whatsoever from an education system which couldn't bend even a bit to help, and even the local doctors had little or no experience of CF.

Chapter 29

The Beginning of the End

I took her into the hospital with her little case; she was not to be in very long. The doctor wanted her to have a few tests while she was in and an X-ray to make sure her lungs were all right for the anaesthetic. I stayed with her all day; she was so used to hospitals that I left her when my brother arrived to take me down to Penicuik, where he and Alice lived then. If she did cry, she didn't let me see. I was to stay with them until May was discharged. There were two other CF children in the ward. Both were very ill, and although they were older than Margaret, they just reminded me of her. They were both sitting up in box-like chairs, all padded to keep them up. They looked like May had looked before we went to Great Ormond Street. I didn't ask about them, but one of the nurses said they were coming on, but then, wouldn't she? May was in for about two days before she had the operation, and by this time, she was 'helping' the nurses. On the day before her operation, she met me at the door of the ward. 'Come and see my wee friend. I am helping the nurses to look after him.' I was quickly led by the hand to one of the cots. May was so full of this baby and desperate for me to look at him. I looked down, and I cannot to this day even begin to describe the poor little baby that was lying in the cot. He had very bad Down's syndrome and was unable to feed. He was being fed by a tube into his tummy, but the nurses were trying to get him to use a spoon, or at least find a way that he could take food from a spoon. All my life, up to that point, I had always believed and, in fact, had said on numerous occasions that I could love and cherish any child. That day I found that I was really a liar. I was so repulsed when I saw that poor little mite that I was deeply ashamed of myself. All my opinion of myself had gone out the window.

May cooed over him and said to me, 'Isn't he lovely? Don't you think he is lovely, Mummy?'

I looked again; all I saw was a wee face like a monkey's with the tongue hanging out, too big for his head. The nurse came along and picked him up, and May sat down on the chair beside the bed. She was given the child to hold. I watched her holding that poor little baby as if he were the most precious baby in the whole world. I was so proud of my daughter and so ashamed of myself.

One never stops learning about oneself. By the time I left in the evening, I had held him, and you could not help being sorry not only for the baby but also for his young parents. His mum looked no more than a girl. May had already made friends with them and told them that he was a good boy. How sad is life for some, I thought. Once again I felt so lucky with May and Andy at home with Granny and Papa. She had her operation and recovered very well. She was getting out on the Monday after the doctors had seen her in the morning and all the results of the tests were back. They were looking at the germs in her mucus in case they required changing her antibiotic, and the results would not be back until then.

On Saturday morning when I went in, the sister was waiting for me. I glanced quickly through the window in the ward door as I had a premonition that something wasn't right. I noticed that neither of the CF children was there; their beds were empty. The sister took me into her office. The ward was being closed as there was an infection in the ward. Some of the children were being transferred to another ward; those like May were being sent home. She was waiting for me in the physiotherapy room. Her case was packed and she was ready to go home. Just at that moment, the doctor came in and explained to me what had happened. The two CF children had passed away, one the previous evening and one during the night. He was very hopeful that May would be all right, but just to make sure, he wanted her out of the hospital and at home. The sister phoned to find out the time of the trains home and when they would arrive in Dundee. Then they phoned Patrick's house and spoke to Alice to tell her that I was going home. My clothes were all at Patrick's, and I think that he must have turned round when he got home and brought my case to the station. I somehow remember him being there when I went on to the train with May. I went to collect May and her case. While I did that, the sister phoned my mum and dad to tell them that I would be on the train and when it would arrive in Dundee. I was put in a taxi, and I was saying my goodbyes and thank you to everyone, and we were on our way home.

It all happened so quickly that I had no time to catch my breath, and that journey from Edinburgh seemed to be the shortest I ever had. When I arrived home, Andy was very pleased to see me and sat on my knee, feeling my face and hair. He was twenty-two months old and a proper toddler. Lots of kisses from me and off he went. He had been very good, Granny said. They had enjoyed looking after him. Every afternoon they walked him to the bowling green, which was on the east end of the town and quite a walk for a little boy of twenty-two months. My mum said that he was so good, he would sit at the bowling green, and he always got an ice cream; so she always had a napkin with her, just in case. Then they would walk home, and he would go out to the garden with Papa and kick a football around until Granny had the tea ready. He was just a joy to be with.

May seemed to be all right; I kept an eye on her very closely, and her breathing didn't seem to be any different from the usual. You have to realise that she was often breathless, but it never seemed to put her up or down unless she had an infection. My mum and dad went home on Sunday. All seemed to be fine, but as May had to go back for a final check-up after her little operation, I could not do anything about us going out to Daddy until after the appointment. On Tuesday afternoon, I was watching out the dining room window while Andy and May were playing some game together. All of a sudden, she collapsed in a heap on the grass. I ran out and saw that she was trying to get her breath and was an awful colour. She was pure white with a tinge of blue around her lips. I knew the sign, and I quickly picked her up and carried her to her bed. Andy was crying as he did not know what was happening. Once I got her on to the bed, I covered her with her tent, filled the humidifier with the glycol and switched it on then I felt for her pulse; I thought it was quite strong. I ran to the phone and contacted the surgery. I asked for a doctor to come immediately as May had collapsed in the garden and was showing signs of heart failure. I rushed back into the bedroom and saw she was no worse. So I picked up Andy and quickly phoned my mum and dad and told them she was ill. They said they would be up as soon as possible and would leave right away. I put Andy down and soothed him, and we sat and waited by her bed for the doctor. He came very quickly, checked her out, and decided to go back to the surgery and phone Edinburgh. He was back in no time at all. He said that the specialist who treated May had told him to leave May with me as I knew what to do better than anyone and to give me all the support I required. By the time he told me that, the chemist arrived with the cylinder of oxygen, which he fixed into her tent. The doctor gave her an injection of an antibiotic that Edinburgh had recommended to give her twice a day for as long as required. My mum and dad arrived and took charge of Andy.

Over next few days, due to the oxygen, the extra antibiotic, and more therapy than usual, she improved. I knew she was not out of danger, but she was eating and looking much better. I began to feel more positive. I was able to get her up out of the oxygen tent for a little bit longer every day until I was able to give her a nice bath. She was taking an interest in Andy and what he was doing and wanted him in to play with her. I was managing fine, so I said to my mum and dad that if they would like to go home and get a breather to please do so. They had come up in such a hurry that Mum just threw some clothes in a bag. They said they would go home, and if I needed them, I was to call and they would come. That night, she had a relapse; she could hardly get any breath at all. She coughed most of the night and was very sick in the early hours. I phoned the doctor in the morning and told him what had happened. He came in and said he would give her another antibiotic orally to be given four times a day. I called my mum, and she said they would just come back and stay. She would pack a case so they wouldn't have to return for anything. I was never so thankful to see them. The next two weeks were a nightmare. Some days I thought she was going to pull through; she was bright, would eat, and then an hour or two later, she would be racked with a cough that had no end and would be fighting for breath. I was doing her therapy, day and night, about every three or four hours, sometimes even less. The doctor or the nurse came in and gave her an injection. She was once again losing weight and she had no muscle to inject the antibiotic into. It was a terrible experience for her and for me. Even my little man would cry when the doctor or nurse came into the house. Even through the closed door he could hear May screaming. I only had one bad hiccup with the doctor. No one came in on the first Saturday evening to give her an injection. I got an apology on the Sunday morning; he had been playing tennis and completely forgot. I was not at all happy and felt let down by him. Her life was hanging by a thread, and he forgot all about her! I never said anything. I was too tired to even try, and I had no time to dwell on things like that. Sometimes in the middle of the night, when she could get no breath and was coughing up nothing, I would just sit and weep. On the third Sunday night, I knew I was not going to be able to save her life. This was one battle too many, and I was losing it. I wouldn't let the doctor, when he came in, give her another injection. If she was to get anything, it had to be by mouth. I was not going to put her through any more pain if I could help it. The doctor wanted me to let her go to Dundee Royal Infirmary. That was where Margaret died. I could never have let her go there. In any case, I was not letting her go into any hospital; when she woke up, the first person she saw had to be me. I did not want her to die alone. I knew she was dying and that no hospital was going to miraculously make it any different. I was adamant; I had been told in the beginning that another illness would be the end. He phoned for his partner, and he came round. They both tried to persuade me, but I knew that I was going to be with her to the end.

In my life, things have happened that I am sure someone somewhere had a hand in them. I call it destiny. Living in Glengate, just two houses away, was the sister of the Chief Specialist of King's Cross Hospital, Dundee where people were sent for barrier nursing and specialist care. My own doctors tried phoning him and found out he was having a meal with his sister. One of the doctors went to the sister's door and explained about May. He came in and sat with me and examined May. He left the room, and I heard him speak on the phone. I thought maybe he was speaking to the doctors in Edinburgh. I heard his voice talking to my mum and dad. When he came in, he asked me to go into the lounge as he wanted to speak to me privately.

'I understand why you don't want to have her taken to the DRI,' he said.

I told him she was not going into a room by herself or in a ward where the nurses did not know her. I did not know how long she had left, but I wanted to make it as good as I could. I wanted it to be as peaceful and full of love as was humanly possible. I had lived with this moment for four years, and I knew what I wanted for my May. I had been told four years ago she might never live outside a hospital, and I had proved them wrong. I had been told that if she took another chest infection which turned into pneumonia, she would not recover. I knew that it had happened. She had been in the wrong place at the wrong time and had picked up an infection on the ward in Edinburgh. I knew it. I had spent years in hospitals.

He said to me, 'Do you understand that she could live in the state she is in now, getting no better but steadily worse, until her heart gave out? There is no way that you could nurse her twenty-four hours a day. You have a beautiful little boy who needs you, and it is reaching the point where it is you or her.' He went on to say, 'I will set up a room for May in King's Cross Hospital. You will have a room right across the corridor from her, and you can be with her all day. And if required, you will be called if she needs you during the night.'

I did realise that I was not in a good shape. I had lost stones in weight. I was never very fat at any time, but I was only about 6st 8lb by that time. I gave in and let them take both of us to the hospital.

An ambulance came for us, and I was so emotional at having to leave Andy behind. I think the last few days had been so bad that I was really at the end of my tether. I could do nothing to relieve her breathing or her cough, and it was soul destroying. The middle of the night was the worst time; it is funny how everything always seems worse then. Then, of course, I had Andy to look after at the same time, and he was often disturbed by the coughing etc. during the night.

Chapter 30

July 1969—The Man on the Moon

She was settled into her bed with oxygen tent and the ability to deliver all her needs, in her own room, and the nurses were so kind and gentle. One of them was a young man, and he had a lot to do with looking after her with me. They had to make sure she did not get bed sores as she had lost a great deal of weight. I had a nice wee room; I just had to look out the door to the right and I could see into her room. It was glass on the outside and glass on to the corridor. The oxygen and glycol helped her breathing, and she had a mask to help get the oxygen into her lungs when she had a coughing spasm. These seemed to get less and less as she got weaker. I no longer was giving her physiotherapy; she didn't have the strength to tolerate them. On Monday morning, my dad contacted the oil company to ask if they could get Alex home as his daughter was very ill and was not expected to survive. They were very good and said they would do everything in their power to get him home as soon as possible. He also phoned Granny Moray to let her know what had happened. Mum and Dad came to see me every day with Andy, who loved nothing better than climbing up on the bed as it was like a climbing frame for him. It was July 1969. Men were travelling to the moon. My dad went into our local TV shop and asked if they could hire me a TV, so I had something to look at during the long hours in the day while I was in the hospital. They were so generous; the manager came himself and fitted it up for me. When children are so ill and they are in a hospital, you have a lot of hours sitting and doing nothing. When you are at home, you are doing everything yourself. The TV was full of pictures and stories of the journey to the moon.

Andy had been saying lots of single words for a long time, but he did not string many together. I think May had spoken for him for the last year and more. When my mum and dad came in, they were always full of what Andy was doing. This day, my mum was full of news. There was a special tune that was played to introduce the programmes about the moon journey. That day

128

when Granny was getting him ready to come to the hospital, he heard the tune being played on the TV and turned to my mum and said in a deep voice, 'The man on the moon.' I had missed his first sentence, but there would be many more high points for which I would be there.

The doctor was right; she never improved, but she still smiled. I read her stories and she watched TV or she lay still, and I wondered if she was still breathing. One morning, one of the young lady doctors passed me as I was going into May's room. She stopped me and, smiling from ear to ear, said, 'She seems to be a lot better today.'

I looked at her and very quietly said, 'I know my child is dying. You don't have to pretend with me.'

She said she was sorry; it was the usual thing to say but she had been off since before May came in. I left her standing there and hoped that she had learnt to find out about the patient and her family before she spoke, as she sounded so patronising. I watched the men land on the moon and have to admit to not being as impressed as I should have been. There they were sending men to the moon, but they couldn't give research money into illnesses like cancer and CF. By the end of the week, I was praying every night for God to take her and give her peace. I watched her life slowly ebb away. I was helpless. No amount of drugs could help her now. It was just a matter of time. On Friday when Mum and Dad came in, she woke up. I got her ice cream, and my mum fed her some. Of course, Andy got some too, and I fed him, or should I say he fed himself. Dad told me that the oil company had been in touch and Alex would be home within a few days. I didn't know whether to be glad or sad. I didn't really want him to see her as she was now; I wanted him to remember her as she was when he was home in January. We had a bad night on Friday night; she was very restless, but by morning, she was more peaceful. I knew that she was slipping away quietly. I phoned my mum and dad and told them not to come. Just about lunchtime a knock came on the outside door, and Alastair came in. He asked how things were, and I said, 'Not good. I don't think she is going to last very much longer.'

He said he would go home and tell his mum that if she wanted to see May, she would need to come quickly. I said that was a good thing to do, and he left saying he would be as quick as he could be. Not long after that, there was another knock and Grandpa Moray came in. It was the first time I had seen him in two years. When he came in, May was having cramps in her legs, and I was massaging them for her. His face was full of emotion. He quietly said he could see I was busy, but he had just found out that May was ill again. He wouldn't stay but left a bunch of flowers and chocolates for me. He gave me a hug, and I think if he had lingered, I would have broken down. I was so pleased to see him. Had things been different, I would have liked to have said to him that I understood why he could not live with Granny Moray, but I never did and I missed my chance.

I settled her down again, and I held her little tiny hand. I don't know how long I sat there quietly with my thoughts. I thought about the long journey we had had over the last four years. I was so frightened that she would suffer in death. Her little body could not sustain any more pain. As I was watching her face, I noticed that she was breathing in her throat, not in her chest. She made a funny little noise, and she quietly passed away. I felt her neck for a pulse, but there was nothing. I bent over her and kissed her little face and told her that it was all over. I told her that she would never have to suffer again and I would never ever forget her as long as I lived. Then I rang the bell.

The male nurse came running in. I said it was all over. He tried speaking to her and worked on her chest for a minute or two. I said to him, 'It's all over. She has gone.' He rang the bell and another nurse came in. They asked me if I wanted a moment on my own with her. I said, 'Just a moment please.' They left me, and I sat quietly weeping. I held her hand and kissed it, and that awful pain in the chest that I had felt when Margaret died came back. Just an empty pain that left you feeling that life would never be the same again. The nurse came back and sat down with me. She asked me if I would be all right. I told her that I had gone through this before. She said she knew; they had been told when May came in. I felt better after she and I had sat for a wee while with my lovely wee girl at peace. I stood up kissed her once more and left the room. I never saw her again. I didn't want to. One can only take so much grief, and to look upon her again would have been too much.

I had just arrived back in my room and was sorting out my bits and pieces, when there was a knock on the door and Alastair and his mum arrived. I told them it was all over. They had been told by a nurse who let them through to my room. Alastair gave me a hug, and I told him that his dad was the last member of the family to see her. I could not believe my ears when Granny Moray spoke. No hug, no kiss, no tears. 'Did he say if he was coming back to me?'

Alastair looked at her and said, 'Mum, what are you thinking about?' They did not linger, and I phoned my mum and dad to tell them about May, and Dad came for me.

Chapter 31

A New Beginning, July 1969

Once I was at home, I had my lovely son to look after, and I put all my energy into him. The next day, a sad thing happened. My mum came to me and asked me if I could speak to my dad; he was in May's room. When I went in, he was lying down on her bed and the tears were pouring down his face. I just sat down beside him and put my arms round him and hugged him. I told him I knew how he felt. He said I didn't. It should have been him, not her, who went. She had all her life to live. I said that she had lived all the life that she had. She was loved more than words could ever express and had left us all with wonderful memories; now we had to put all our energies into Andy. We were lucky, and we had to remember that. He gradually got control of himself, and I said that May wouldn't have liked to see him upset. I told him to just remember the happy times. He got up, said I was right, and we both left the room. I had my arms round him, and Andy came running out to look for him and he went off with his wee grandson.

I started the arrangements for the funeral and the notice for the papers and hoped that Alex would arrive this time before it was all over. He did arrive two days before and never mentioned May but busied himself with Andy. He also arranged for a lovely wreath, shaped like a heart, of pink carnations from Mummy, Daddy, and Andy, and saw to all the details of the death certificate. Mr Sturrock brought her coffin home the night before her funeral, and it lay on her bed. He also brought her silver bracelet, which I put away safely. I know that at sometime during that evening my mum and dad and Alex and myself quietly visited her and said our personal goodbyes. When I went in, I said to myself, 'Another small white coffin, another beloved child.' The cards and letters started to appear in bundles, even before the notice was in the *Courier*. Alex and I were overwhelmed by the amount of mail. Somehow I read them at the time, but they didn't upset me; that came later. We had a small service in the house; it was not by my old minister but the new one in Mum and Dad's church, who really didn't know Alex and me. Then we travelled to Dundee

Crematorium. It was a lovely funeral; the music was lovely, and though it broke my heart, during the service I was able to recover again very quickly. I was glad to see Papa Moray there as I knew how much he had loved her.

We had been so busy with everything that it wasn't until the night of the funeral that Alex and I were alone. I was lying in bed, and I started to weep. He stopped me.

He said, 'Don't cry. We have cried all our tears when she was alive. We will not cry for her now. She is at peace.' He never spoke about her after that at all. It was as if she had not existed. I understood. I knew that if he talked about her, he would break down and he didn't want that to happen. I had seen my dad and didn't want the same to happen to Alex, but I did think that at some time he would speak about her and all the things she had done and all the laughter she had shared and the love she had spread around her. But he never did.

After Margaret's death, it was as if my brain had switched off with the shock. No one was prepared for it; no one was looking for anything like that to happen at all until the last two days, when the bottom fell out of our lives. It was different with May's death. I had lived with it for nearly four years and the anxiety I had felt over her precarious health because of the CF. I became the sole provider of her therapy, medicines, and diet. The responsibility for her life was in my hands. Once I left Great Ormond Street and Tadworth Court, I was on my own. I never had the same faith in the hospitals or the doctors in Scotland. In Iran, I had 100 per cent help, but still the responsibility lay with me. These things are bad enough in themselves, but take into account that I was alone—no family when in Iran, no husband when in Scotland, and when in England, there was no one of my own at all. I had lived with May and for May every day for all that time, with very little break, until Andy came into my life. Now I had to learn to live without her by my side, sharing Andy with me, my wee buddy and pal. I knew it was going to take me a long time before my brain and my heart healed from the pain I felt. I knew I wasn't alone in my sorrow for I knew my parents were suffering too. However, that night a wedge came between Alex and me, which stayed there for many months.

We were up to the eyes getting everything ready to go back together to Iran. Tickets and visas for Andy and me had to be sent from London. I had been buying all summer, a dress here and a skirt there, so I actually had all my clothes ready to take out. I had also bought for Andy. Funnily enough, I had not bought very much for May. Had I had a premonition? Or maybe I didn't want to tempt fate. We gave what she had to a charity shop in town. We also gave her humidifier to the Surgery in Kirrriemuir. One of my worries after May's death was how my lovely wee man would take her not being there. They were inseparable; everywhere she went, he went. She had been playing with him all his life, and she was at home more than other siblings were. I just hoped he would not miss her too much. He never once mentioned May, and I never mentioned her to him. His age was his saviour, he was mine.

One good thing happened which helped us to get our life back to as normal as it could be under the circumstances. Edna and Peter Mullet and Lesley were coming up to stay two days after the funeral for a holiday. They would be leaving the day we left for Iran, to go touring Scotland. I know it really helped us, as we took them all over the place—up the Glens and down to Glamis and we just had a happy time. Lesley thought Andy was wonderful. He just happened to have his second birthday then, so we had a wee tea party with a cake for him. Granny Moray came, but as Peter and Edna were there, she was unable to talk about herself or May. It was Andy's day, and we made it as good as we could for him. It was good for my mum and dad to meet Peter and Edna and Lesley, and it did help them when we left, as Edna and Peter were taking us down to Dundee and then coming back to the house for lunch before they went off. It meant my mum and dad were busy after we left.

Chapter 32

A New Journey in Life; Iran, 1969-1970

It was funny, just the three of us—me and my boys. Alex was so good with Andy, who was really a man's boy, as my dad had been his life when I was busy with May. He didn't like giving kisses; men don't kiss, do they?

We had a nice journey out to Abadan. We stopped over as usual in London and had a meal in the hotel in the evening and took Andy with us. He sat like a little man and behaved very well. I was looking forward to my new house. My third home in Iran.

We arrived in the evening, and Alex carried Andy down the steps of the plane. As we walked over the tarmac to the Arrivals building, I saw Peter, Gill and the young minister of the church standing, waiting for us. They were waving at us. I lifted my hand and waved back. I said to myself, 'I have come home.' There was something rather sad in the fact that I felt like that on that night. Although I was a member of one of the churches in Kirriemuir, I had not had time to actually go to the services. However, I had met the young minister in the street after May died. He introduced himself to me. He apologised for not coming to see me and making himself known to me, as obviously I had not been able to attend church because of the circumstance I was in. I said it didn't matter and no apologies were necessary. It wasn't until I saw Dan waiting at the airport that I felt that somehow something had been missing.

Hugs and kisses all round and we were off in the taxi to our new home. As it was practically the same as our previous one, it didn't seem too strange, the only difference being we were on the right side of a semi-detached house instead of the left. When we got in, Shona Macintosh was waiting for us. The lounge was full of flowers—quite beautiful but very moving. I felt that I was walking into a mausoleum, not my lounge. No one stayed very long, and as we had been travelling all day, it was just as well. Andy was sleeping on his feet, poor wee soul. He always travelled well, but he knew nothing else and just took it in his stride. I bathed him and fed him and popped him into bed. Alex had to work the next day, so he wasn't long in following him. Once Jabber had cleared up and gone off to his house in the compound at the back, I pottered about that night for ages. I was too wound up to sleep. My head was in a spin. Eventually, I went off to bed and slept the sleep of the dead.

When I woke up, the house was so quiet and peaceful. I got out of bed and went to see if Andy was awake. He wasn't in his room, and I looked at the time and realised it was nearly 11 a.m. He was in the kitchen with Jabber, all dressed and fed. His little bike was in the compound, and he was popping in and out the door, up and down the steps—quite the thing. I need not have worried about him. Once I was ready, we went shopping to the Staff Store. I didn't want to stay in as I didn't feel strong enough mentally for too many visitors. Shona had said before she left the night before that 'we will be in to see you'. However, if they came, I needed to bake and have something to offer them. My new house was so near the Staff Store I could go out the back garden gate and walk over the bridge over the water ditch and I would be there. However, I always walked round by the road with Andy. It was a case of coming out of the driveway gates and turning left and then left again almost immediately, then up to the next junction and turn left again, and hey presto, there was the Staff Store—no problems when you forgot the item you went in for but came home with things you hadn't meant to buy. After lunch, when Jabber had gone off for his break, I put Andy down for a sleep and that was when I realised how my life had changed. I was on my own with nothing to do for the first time in months. I had time to think; I can remember so clearly all that had happened over that period from the middle of June to that August day even now. I think that afternoon was the start of my grieving for May; up to that point, I had been busy with everything going on about me, but that afternoon, life stood still for the first time. I felt that I was so alone in the world and that Andy could manage without me. He had been looked after most of the previous month and much longer on and off by Granny and Papa, and now Jabber had taken over. I know now that I was depressed and sorry for myself, but I just wept. I crept about the house looking for anything belonging to May, and all I found tucked in a drawer was photographs of her that Alex had put away. The only thing of hers, which now belonged to Andy, was the wee bike. I felt that no one cared that she had died or that I had lost my most beloved little girl. How could God be so cruel and take both my girls from me?

Of course, I exhausted myself, and I fell asleep on the settee in the lounge. I woke up with Andy standing in front of me. I just lifted him up and hugged him to me and went into the garden where I played with him on his bike until teatime. By the time Alex came home, Andy was ready for bed, so he didn't have his dad for long in the evenings.

Each day was mostly like that. Things had changed in Abadan; some of the older captains and engineers had been retired, and that is how we got our house and our dog. Tojo was known to us as he had lived across the road from our last home with one of the engineers who was retiring. We were in the habit of looking after him when his owner was on leave. Tom, the cat, had decided he wanted to stay around our old home, and after trying to get him to stay in his new home without success, as he kept escaping and going back, our old neighbour, an Iranian doctor, said, 'Please just leave him here. We feed him anyway and the children love him.' So he stayed and Tojo arrived. He was a cross of a Miniature German Schnauzer and a Jack Russell. He was quite a character and about three or four years old. Unfortunately, there was only one other expatriate on our side of the main road, and I felt a bit out on a limb.

Before May's death, when in I was in Abadan, I had been so busy I never joined any of the clubs. Life, when not with Alex, had been made up of visiting the ladies around the area for coffee. Those ladies were nearly all away. I decided to join the Church Charity Work Group. They made items to sell at a big sale once a year, and they met in the church hall every Monday. The money went to a clinic based up, as far as I can remember, in the north-east of Iran. There was no National Health Service, and the British couple who ran it totally relied on charity money. So off I went and left Jabber in charge of Andy, who enjoyed himself as one of Jabber's daughters had come to visit, so he had another person to dote on him. When Alex came in that evening he asked me how I got on.

'Well,' I said, 'I think it is a therapy session for expatriate women. I was given an empty paper hanky box, which I had to reinforce with card. Then when it dried, I was given a bag of pasta, which I had to stick on the box with UHU glue. Apart from being high on the glue, it was fine. I made three boxes, so I think I was quite away with the fairies by the time I finished as the designs on the boxes got worse as the morning progressed. I get to spray them gold next week and add red ribbons and a candle.'

He just laughed. I think he was worrying about me, but we seemed to have lost the art of talking to each other. We pussyfooted around each other. The wedge was still there; I yearned to be cuddled and kissed, but a barrier remained.

One afternoon when Andy was having his nap, I was sitting quietly in the lounge. The only noise was the air conditioning unit which, after a while, seemed to disappear into the background. My thoughts wandered over the last few years, and as usual, they were very much on these last weeks of May's life. I really hadn't had a lot of time to sit and think. I thought about the six years we had had her and how we were so lucky that she lived to be a couple of weeks off her sixth birthday. After all, the doctors had thought she would never come out of hospital or be able to live as normal a life as she had. It struck like a bolt of lightning that her death could have been avoided. In Great Ormand Street, the CF children were in a dedicated ward, and in Tadworth Court, they were with asthmatic and diabetic children. Why were the CF children in Edinburgh in an open ward? May had been allowed to play with children and hold a baby who was visited by outsiders. Where had the infection come from? How did the infection get into the ward, and who brought it in? Were the cleaners less than diligent? Were the nurses up to scratch with their hygiene? May died because she picked up an infection in a children's hospital, where she should have been safe. I started to feel very angry. All that we had gone through, May, Alex my parents, and I, trying to keep her alive, so she could be killed in a hospital! That was the deepest cut of all, I felt. The anger, of course, didn't last, but it did help me channel my grief away from sorrow for a little while. I never mentioned my thoughts to anyone as I knew we had to live with her death and nothing would bring her back again. I am sure that if it happens in this day and age, the parents will be up in arms and sue the hospital for bad practice.

Life took on the same pattern; the 'ladies' never did come to visit. They probably didn't know what to say to me so stayed away. On Fridays, Alex played golf in the morning and Andy and I joined him for lunch and stayed for a while, meeting the teachers and some other ladies I knew from the tug staff and the church. If he played in the afternoon, we went up at around 4.30 p.m., just as we had done when May was alive. We would then either go to the Super's house for a buffet tea with the 'boys' and their girlfriends or we came home after having a meal at the Golf Club. Sometimes, Alex took Andy when he went for his Sunday papers (on a Friday) to the IPA shop, which also sold beer and, for Andy, a Coke float (Coke and ice cream). After lunch, we would go to the Karting Club as we had done when May was with us. Jabber's day off was on Friday, and he usually went to his home in the village, a terrible place with no sanitation and houses made of mud and corrugated roofs. It is difficult to explain, but Jabber's wife did not like him working for a woman, especially a non-Muslim. It had been different when I wasn't living there; she came regularly with the girls and stayed for weeks, but whenever I appeared, off she went. However, the girls were allowed to come and stay.

Chapter 33

More Good News

I wrote my letters home every week, and at that time I wrote to the adoption society to tell them that May had lost her battle with CF. I hadn't told Alex I had written as I was just letting them know. Mrs Cunningham and the girls in the office were always interested in us, and every Christmas, I wrote a long letter to them all, giving them news of Andy and May. When I received a reply, I was astounded to read that if we wished for another baby, 'to let them know'. If the answer was yes and if I came home in February, we would be given the chance to adopt again. I wasn't sure how Alex would react; we were quite far apart in our relationship with each other. On the surface, when we were with Andy or in company, we appeared as if everything was the same as before May's death, but in reality, we weren't. This news was, for me, the very thing to help me put the past months behind me and soften May's death. I knew I would never forget her, but she would be in her right place in my heart, not the overwhelming feeling that I had had for weeks. I had to wait until Alex came home from work to find out what he thought. I prayed to God that he would feel like me and want another baby. We had never had any problem accepting Andy as our own; he was ours, heart and soul, and we loved him as much, if not more, in some ways than if I had given birth as we never took his life for granted. I had been given a card with a verse on it, when I first adopted, from a friend of my mum's. It was written from a mother to her adopted child. It said

> Never forget, not for a minute
> Though you weren't born under my heart
> You were born in it.

I always felt that it was so true, for we didn't feel any difference between our feelings for Margaret and May and our feelings for Andy. We loved him with all our heart.

When Alex came in quite a bit later than normal—so Andy was already in his bed—I handed him the letter to read, and I left him alone. He came very quietly into the bedroom where I was and put his arms around me and turned me to face him. I looked up into his face and saw a look that had been missing for weeks. He said that if it was all right with me, he would love to have another child. I just kissed him and hugged him, and the wedge just disappeared. I thought he would never let me go; all the pent-up emotion of the last few months welled up inside, and my love for my gentle Alex overwhelmed me. Much later that evening, Alex said he was over the moon and was in total agreement that we should have another baby. We would not say what we wanted, a boy or a girl. Any child would be a gift, a surprise, as we had never even thought—either of us—that we would be eligible for another child. I agreed. 'Let us wait and see what happens in February.' I wrote back immediately and said a big yes, and a *thank you*. The next night when he came home, it was the old Alex, a kiss for me and a cuddle for his wee man, and when Andy was fed and bedded, we sat down to our meal. He sat very quietly eating his meal and was deep in thought, but looked content. Once he was finished, he went off out. I watched him going into a taxi and was on tenterhooks until he came back. He brought back a bunch of flowers and a gold pendant from the bazaar. He handed them to me and took me in his arms and said he was sorry if he had hurt me and he loved me. He said that Andy and I were all he wanted and that our new baby would make our life complete again. Although he still had to work all day, and often he worked quite late, he had time for us when he came home. He still drank his beer, but our life got better and better, and after all we had gone through, I did feel loved again.

One day, Peter came to visit me; he had a proposition for me to think about. He was a member of the Theatre Club and was about to produce a farce *The Middle Watch*. The leading man was not very tall, and they were having difficulty in finding a small man to play his Chinese servant. Would I be interested in doing it? I looked at the part, and it did not seem to me to be too long or difficult. I had not been on stage since I was a child playing the piano. However as a prospective trainer for Guiding, I was used to standing up in front of people and delivering a talk or an interesting training. I spoke to Alex, and, although he was not in the least bit interested in theatre, he said I ought to have a go. I did, and I thoroughly enjoyed my first of the many appearances on the stage of the Little Theatre in Abadan. It opened new doors, and I made new friends. I appeared in two productions before Christmas; the second was an *Old time Review*, and I was busy with that as well. I was starting the show, singing a musical song and had to make myself a Victorian skirt and top. It was a bawdy Victorian music hall song but just the thing to set the evening off. I also made the costumes, found the music, and choreographed four of the auditors from the external audit firm who were to be Belly dancers. Four others were making up a band behind them, suitably attired. The dancers were sensational, two being very large and nothing like belly dancers. It was all fun, and I did enjoy myself. Peter had a great notion to have me star in *The Prime of Miss Jean Brodie*. However, as I was going home in February for my very special, new baby, he would have to wait until I came back.

One Friday afternoon when we were unable to go anywhere for the weather, no golf no karting, I realised I hadn't seen Alex for a while. Andy was having his rest, and I thought maybe that was what Alex was doing. After a while, I became curious, so I went to find him. I went quietly in case he was asleep. When I looked into the bedroom, he was standing in front of the tallboy, where he had placed all the photographs of May that used to sit about the house. He was looking at them one by one, over and over again. He did not see me, so I moved quietly away and went into the kitchen, put on the kettle, and made a bit of noise before going through. He was still standing in front of the tallboy, but the drawer was shut. I asked him if he would like a cup of coffee, and he said, 'No, I will have a beer.' I will never know if he had been crying, but I knew that hiding the photos was not the way forward. When he was at work the next day, I took out the photographs and placed two of them back in the places they had always sat before. When he came in from work, he never mentioned them and I did not say a word. I knew that he was still like me, coming to terms with our loss.

The church bazaar was just before Christmas. I have to say that even though I was not initially impressed by the craftwork I was doing, by the time they were finished, some of them were really lovely. All were Christmas-related in bright red, gold green, and silver. We also sold cake and candy and clothes and books—in fact, the usual things you would see at a church bazaar at home—and it was a great success. The Iranian ladies of all shapes and backgrounds came in there droves.

Christmas 1969 was a good time with parties for Andy and for us; he enjoyed himself. He went to the Golf Club party where Santa Claus arrived by helicopter. Great was the excitement. I have to say that you would not have believed we were in a Muslim country. The Golf Club had a mixed nationality membership. The Iranians were there, enjoying our Christmas as much as we were. Their children got their presents from Santa, just like our own. I had an old Christmas tree I had brought from home, and it came out again along with the decorations. I never really managed to make the lounge very Christmassy, but Andy didn't care; he loved it anyway and knew no better.

Hogmanay was a great night at the Golf Club. There was a lovely buffet meal and dancing with some music to remind us that it was a Scottish evening. I did enjoy myself very much. I did have a little hiccup when the bells rang at twelve o'clock. We had a countdown to midnight, but I was very quiet as I had a lump in my throat, the size of a golf ball.

Chapter 34

A New Beginning, and a New Life

We left Abadan on a VC10 on 3 February 1970; Andy was two and a half years old. We were able to fly straight to London. All the omens were good. We left Alex happy and looking forward to coming home and, hopefully, to his new baby. Andy and I stayed in London—not at the airport, but actually in London itself. He was out for the count by the time we got into the hotel, and I just laid him down on a chair as I booked in and carried him up in the lift and into the room. I gently removed his duffle coat and trousers and put him in the double bed. Once I was settled myself, I got room service and had a good cup of tea and something to eat. I got a sandwich and milk for Andy as I had a feeling he would wake up hungry, and he did at about midnight. So he had a midnight feast, and I had more tea. In the morning, after a bath—he was looking his best—we had breakfast in the dining room. We had an appointment with Mrs Cunningham at 11 a.m. We took a taxi to the office and went in. She was so pleased to see us and to meet Andy again. The last time she saw him, he was six weeks old. The others in the office also came to see him, and the girls were amazed at him. He spoke about being on the VC10 and how it went straight into the air, all with lots of hand and arm movement. They asked him about the food and he was telling them all about the meal he had and his midnight feast. Mrs Cunningham then told me that there were two boys ready for adoption. They were both older than six weeks, and one of them was half Iranian. I could see trouble if I returned to Iran with a baby who had Iranian blood, even if he was legally ours. She then gave me the news that a little girl had been born yesterday, on 3 February, at 6 p.m. I told her that was the time we arrived at Heathrow, a coincidence, was it not? She had been to see her and she was a pretty little one, weighing in at 6lb. She was already with foster carers until the time she could come to me if I wanted her. I was given a provisional date and asked if I would manage to come for her. One of the office girls told me quietly that Mrs Cunningham was retiring and she wasn't doing so until she had seen Alex and me with our new daughter. She had told them, having met my mum and dad, about the kindness she got from them when she brought up Andy and how she admired Alex and me and the courage we had shown. She just had to do this special one. I told the girl that we thought the world of her as she done so much for us and been so helpful. After a cup of tea with them all, we left for Heathrow to get the plane to Edinburgh and the long haul home to Kirriemuir.

The welcome was the usual from Mum and Dad. Dad was at the station to meet us, and Mum was at the door when we arrived. Then it was all go as we had to get everything ready for the new baby. Andy and I went down to Dundee for a few days, and Granny and I had a good shopping spree. I had given away my lovely coach pram, so I bought a lightweight folding pram. It was the same make as the coach pram, so it was a good one. It had a hood and an apron, but I could fold it up to get it in a car or when travelling by plane. It was a bit big for her to begin with, so Alice gave me the carrycot that she had got for John. Then May had used it, then Margaret, then Andy, and then her second boy, David, who was coming up to one year. As she was not having any more children, I could keep it and take it out with me.

The six weeks just flew past, and before we knew it, I was organising myself for the big day to fly from Dundee to Edinburgh, Edinburgh to Gatwick and return by the late afternoon flight. I left Kirriemuir on 17 March. Dad took me to Dundee and would be there for me when I got back. I was carrying the cot, a bag with a shawl and container for the bottles etc., and a plastic bag for the nappies. The plane at Dundee Airport held four people, but only two others were with me on the journey to Edinburgh. I then got a flight to Gatwick and a train to London and a taxi to the office. They were waiting for me, and after the usual greetings and questions about Andy, I was taken into a room on my own. Mrs Cunningham brought in the tiniest baby I had held and by far the smallest of my two. I was left with her and told that if I didn't want her, I could just let them know. She was a lovely little dainty baby, but let us be honest—it wouldn't have mattered what she was like; I wanted her. I inspected her all over and kissed her wee fingers and her toes and cuddled her, and she just lay in my arms and accepted it with a gurgle. I told Mrs Cunningham when she came back into the room, 'I had no choice when I gave birth, so why get a choice now?' In any case, I wanted her more than they all could imagine. We had decided to call any baby girl we were lucky enough to get, Helen. May had been flower girl at Helen's wedding, and Helen had been one of my bridesmaids. The bag was filled with a change of nappies and two bottles and extra SMA and bibs, enough to get me home. A taxi was called, and there were good wishes from everyone. All of them were at the door to wave us off. There is always a hitch when you travel with a baby, and it started off because I did not have an English note in my purse and the driver wasn't happy. On arrival at the train station, I was wondering what I would do as he didn't want my Scottish £10 note. In the end, he let me off free. The train was busy as it was commuter time, and I had to stand to begin with, carrycot and all, until a man gave me a seat. Helen had started to become restless, and I was feeling a bit stressed. When we got into the Departure lounge I realised we had to walk over the tarmac to get on the plane. The carrycot was now in the baggage hold but carrying a restless baby and a pretty heavy holdall is not ideal; however, there was a coloured gentleman who carried my bag on to the plane for me. Helen came into my life, letting the world know she was there. She cried all the way from Gatwick to Edinburgh. She was hanging from a sky cot, and I asked the stewardess if she would heat up a bottle for me. She did so after I had asked twice more for it, and I was fizzing by the time she brought it. Once I had fed her, she settled down in my arms, but when I put her into the sky cot for landing, she started up again. I had been used to the sky cot being at the front of a plane sitting on a shelf, all fastened down for safety, not one swinging about from the ceiling. I was so upset one way and another that when I was leaving the plane, I told the stewardesses, who were smiling and charming the men leaving the plane, that I would never fly Caledonian Airways again. I had travelled thousands of miles in a year with small babies and children and had never experienced such unhelpful stewardesses in my travelling life. Then it was back on the small plane to Dundee, which was fine and quite a shock for the pilot. He asked me very quietly, 'You didn't have the bundle with you this morning?'

I just smiled and said, 'This is Helen Moray. She is an instant baby. You put the powder into a basin, mix, and out pops a baby.' By the time I climbed into my dad's car, I was tired, but extremely happy. If I was really good with words, I could, maybe, give you some idea of how I felt. All our dreams had come true. We were so lucky, as we never had even thought that we would ever be given an opportunity to adopt another child, let alone a baby girl. Andy was so excited about his little sister and had to examine her well and cuddle her before he going to bed. Granny and Papa stayed for a few days, but I was lucky she was a good baby, always smiling and happy, but didn't like sleeping in the evening. I gave up trying and decided that I would wait until her daddy came home in April and there was only us to distract her. However, when he did come home, he was no more successful than I was and so we had a lovely little baby who kept us company every evening, when we were sitting watching the TV. We were once again a couple, very happy in each other's company, and loving in every way. I had so missed the physical side of my marriage when Alex and I seemed so far apart and trying to come to terms with May's death. We enjoyed our new baby very much, and Andy just loved helping her get a bath. It helped him greatly having her there, and she watched him all the time. We were a family again, and this time we did not have the pressure that May's life had put on us, physically and mentally. It was great being a family, and although our house was still the hub for family and friends to visit, we were able to get about ourselves as we hired a car for Alex's leave. This time for the adoption, we had the one visit to the house for the court, but as it was only a little over two and a half years since we had gone through it all, it was just a formality. My solicitor was as good as his word and said he would try to get the adoption through as quickly as possible after Alex had lived four weeks with her. By the time Alex left again in May, we were hopeful of being with him by the end of July or the beginning of August. We still had all the butterflies in the stomach that we experienced when waiting for the adoption to go to court. Alex left in a great frame of mind and in anticipation of welcoming the three of us in a couple of months. His lovely little flower was blossoming before his eyes, as well as his little man—who was his shadow.

Once Alex left, I was not as unhappy as I had been in the past as he had left in an upbeat manner, just talking about when we would be together again in a few weeks. I was so happy and so busy; there was no time to think of anything but looking after my lovely children. It was not easy with a baby and a two-year-old, but somehow one managed. After my previous experiences, anything was easier. When it came to bedtime, I slept like a log as I was once again so tired, but happy and content. Of course, there were nights when sleep was dictated by one or other of the little ones, but it was nothing compared with my time with Margaret and May and when Andy was small.

On the 14 July 1970, the Open Championship was going on at the old course, St Andrews. I came down from Kirriemuir to Dundee the day before, and it was decided that we would have a day of visiting family in St Andrews and go to see the golfers at the eighteenth hole. I was just getting the baby bag filled with all that was required, when around 9.30 a.m., the phone at my mum's rang. It was my solicitor to say that Helen's adoption had gone through that morning, and everything would be in the post by tomorrow. I thanked him over and over again, and when I put the phone down, I just jumped for joy. My dad and mum were standing in the hall, and their expressions were of utter relief and joy. My dad once again was all over Helen, making sure she was safe in the car and her cot in the boot. He had to carry her out to the car. Once again, he had never touched her until she was his own *granddaughter*. We had a wonderful day with coffee with our lady relations, and then I was off to the park to let Andy play on the swings. When it came to lunchtime and I went to feed Helen, I realised that I had not put any teats into the bottles of milk. My dad went ballistic. How stupid was I? Of course, what had happened, when the phone rang, I had been working on the bottles and had completely forgotten to put the teats inside the lids. I had to run all the way to Boots the

Chemist in St Andrews to buy the teats I required for her bottles. It was easy to see that her grandpa was fully on board with his granddaughter.

Helen's adoption and her coming into our lives changed us forever. She was everything we ever wanted. We never once thought of comparing her with either Margaret or May as she was a little person from the very beginning. A little one-off, a joy, a treasure to be loved, and we did love her so very much. We never took Andy's life for granted, and we were the same with Helen. They were gifts given to us to keep and cherish as our own, and we did.

I immediately phoned the oil company and the travel agents and made all the arrangements for our return. The journey back to Abadan wasn't easy with a six-month-old baby and a three-year-old, Andy having his birthday just days before we left Kirriemuir. The amount of cases, prams, and bags was unbelievable. Helen wasn't happy at Heathrow, London, as it was so noisy, and everyone wanted to speak to the both of them. They were blond and lovely children and very attractive to look at and, I have to say, to be with. Helen cried until we got on the plane, and although she didn't sleep, she was quiet. Andy slept through most of the journey. I had chosen a night flight thinking it would be better for us, and it was. Somehow with all that had gone before, this journey was easier than I expected, and I was all excited to be seeing Alex again. He, of course, was waiting for us once I and the children were through immigration and customs, which by now, as you can imagine, I was getting used to. There he was to gather up our luggage and cot and its wheels plus our folding pram etc., etc. The taxi was waiting for us, and we bundled everything into it and went home. The Moray family was complete at last, and the future all theirs.